T0277543

PRAISE FOR
CAUGHT IN THE CROSSHAIRS
OF AMERICAN HEALTHCARE

"Dr. Sederer models a rare combination of clinical expertise, executive savvy, eloquence, and old-fashioned compassion as he recounts a dramatic story of leading clinically necessary change in a revered but fraying hospital. This book should be required reading for anyone who wants to understand transformational leadership."

—*Donald M. Berwick, MD, MPP,* President Emeritus and Senior
Fellow, Institute for Healthcare Improvement

"What happens when a venerable old hospital must come into modern healthcare or die? *Caught in the Crosshairs of American Healthcare* tells the story. Sederer had been hired to help prevent the renowned McLean Psychiatric Hospital from closing. The corporatization of medicine was engulfing it with drastic cuts in payment and it was on a downward spiral of losing money. It wasn't as impossible a task as it might have been, though, because Sederer knew that McLean's long-term model of psychiatric care was counterproductive. What worked in psychiatry was rapid medical treatment, family involvement, and team care. It took six years but, in the end, McLean succeeded, and today the beautiful old hospital is still open and has maintained its unique place in psychiatry, with the triple mission of clinical care, training, and research. We need more of such successes."

—*Victoria Sweet, MD, PhD,* best-selling author of
God's Hotel and *Slow Medicine*

"Most of us want to relate to healthcare on the most personal of terms—'seeing' the doctor in moments intimate and private. In *Caught in the Crosshairs of American Healthcare*, Dr. Sederer reveals the interlocking system of for-profit corporate policies and practices that makes us feel small, alone, and helpless. He uses a case study of saving a Harvard hospital, where he was Chief Medical Officer, by providing science-based clinical care so that patients, like you and me, families and hospitals too, come first—not profits."

—*Monsignor Donald Sakano*, priest, Archdiocese of New York

"Lloyd Sederer is not only one of our nation's most storied public health psychiatrists, he is a masterclass storyteller. Sederer spins the tale of the near-sinking of the famed McLean Hospital in the wake of managed care's torpedoing American healthcare and its rescue by instating research-backed clinical models of care. An illuminating book for anyone concerned about people suffering from psychiatric illnesses and the ideas and forces shaping their care."

—*Lisa Gornick, PhD*, author of *Ana Turns* and *The Peacock Feast*

"Psychiatrist, problem solver, prolific author, and captivating story-teller—that's Dr. Lloyd Sederer. *Caught in the Crosshairs of American Healthcare*—Lloyd's fourteenth book—is the story of how corporate, profit-driven insurance companies now dominate American medicine, to the detriment of patients, families, and hospitals. He uses a Harvard teaching hospital where he served as medical director as a case study of how to survive, then prosper, holding to compassionate, accessible, equitable, and science-based care."

—*Lipi Roy, MD, MPH, FASAM*, physician, national addiction medicine expert, and media medical commentator

CAUGHT *in the* CROSSHAIRS *of* AMERICAN HEALTHCARE

LLOYD I. SEDERER, MD

GREENLEAF
BOOK GROUP PRESS

This book is intended as a reference volume only, not as a medical manual. The information given here is designed to help you make informed decisions about your health. It is not intended as a substitute for any treatment that may have been prescribed by your doctor. If you suspect that you have a medical problem, you should seek competent medical help. You should not begin a new health regimen without first consulting a medical professional.

Published by Greenleaf Book Group Press
Austin, Texas
www.gbgpress.com

Distributed by Greenleaf Book Group

For ordering information or special discounts for bulk purchases, please contact Greenleaf Book Group at PO Box 91869, Austin, TX 78709, 512.891.6100.

Design and composition by Greenleaf Book Group
Cover design by Greenleaf Book Group
Cover Images: ©iStockphoto/porcorex and ©iStockphoto/FGorgun

Publisher's Cataloging-in-Publication data is available.

Print ISBN: 979-8-88645-129-0

eBook ISBN: 979-8-88645-130-6

To offset the number of trees consumed in the printing of our books, Greenleaf donates a portion of the proceeds from each printing to the Arbor Day Foundation. Greenleaf Book Group has replaced over 50,000 trees since 2007.

Printed in the United States of America on acid-free paper

24 25 26 27 28 29 30 31   10 9 8 7 6 5 4 3 2 1

First Edition

CONTENTS

1

LANDING ZONE

Early on a rainy, spring Monday morning in 1989, fueled by black coffee and a banana, I boarded my old Subaru hatchback. Instead of driving to Cambridge, where I had worked for the previous seven years, I drove to Belmont, Massachusetts, just west and a little north of Cambridge. My new commute would take no more than twenty minutes, all on surface streets, with little traffic.

When you approach Belmont from any direction on the compass, it's soon clear this is a prosperous town—not because of McLean Hospital but because it is a lovely residential community. There are good-sized homes set on well-tended, spacious lots with two- and three-car garages. It is a perfect suburban home, if you can afford it.

McLean Hospital is not far from Belmont's main street, with its array of shops and services. To get to the hospital, however, a driver (there was no bus) had to find Mill Street and snake up a large hill. The hospital is on the right but barely visible, behind dense shrubs and trees abutting the inside of its tall metal fence. A small wood-framed house, a residence for patients, sits immediately after the entrance. Across from this lodge is a marker: a massive granite boulder signaling your right turn onto the grounds, where you ascend even farther onto the massive campus, as well as farther from the reality of the town.

The McLean Hospital logo is cut into the granite stone, announcing you have arrived. Imagine the vast range of reactions at that moment. A family at its wit's end bringing a loved one, adult and child, for admission; employees of all stripes, junior and senior doctors; residents and fellows; research scientists; a few botanists; nurses; social workers; psychologists; aides; groundskeepers; cafeteria workers; housekeeping; and many others—for decades, they all passed this stone, every day.

McLean Hospital, at the time of my hire, had prided itself in providing longer term, inpatient care. Even well into the twentieth century, there were patients who stayed in the hospital for years. Some were on locked inpatient units, and others were in the collection of open, residential buildings, all but one on the campus. Long-term treatment, particularly psychoanalytic psychotherapy (a derivative of psychoanalysis), had generally been considered the standard of good care for people with serious mental illnesses. Not only for clinical depression and traumatic conditions, but also for those suffering from schizophrenia and bipolar disorder.

Not so anymore. There has been no research evidence supporting long-term, inpatient psychotherapy. It also carries the risk of triggering regression in patients.[1] Mental healthcare has moved on

---

1   R. E. Drake and L. I. Sederer, "The Adverse Effects of Intensive Treatment of Chronic Schizophrenia," *Comprehensive Psychiatry* 27, no. 4 (1986): 313–326.

R. E. Drake and L. I. Sederer, "Inpatient Psychotherapy of Chronic Schizophrenia: Avoiding Regression," *Hospital Community Psychiatry* 37 (1986): 897–901.

to more proven, evidence-based treatments, but fixed beliefs often defy change.

When I drove past the granite marker, you could say I had arrived metaphorically, as well as physically: I was stepping up to a higher station in my professional career. McLean was a Harvard teaching hospital, but I had already worked in several—one was Massachusetts General (MGH)—arguably the most prominent and iconic of the Harvard medical fleet. Like McLean, MGH had served Boston, then the United States, and then the world, for 180 years.

The original McLean Hospital was chartered in 1811 (as was MGH) and located in Charlestown, now a part of Somerville, Massachusetts. When the railroad arrived later in the nineteenth century, McLean had to be moved. In 1895, the newly built McLean opened in Waverley (now Belmont), adjacent to Cambridge and not far from Boston proper.

In the mid-nineteenth century, McLean had become one of the nation's limited number of psychiatric hospitals providing "moral therapy." Moral therapy came to the US principally from Britain, to be adopted by notable psychiatric hospitals, including McLean. It promoted treating patients with dignity and respect and keeping them occupied with "purposeful activities."

Moral therapy was a clear humane step away from the institutional neglect that had characterized mental hospitals since the late eighteenth century. A robust schedule of "purposeful activities" (e.g., farming, cooking, landscape maintenance) was believed to be beneficial, therapeutic, on the basis of its use in the United Kingdom. It seemed to offer the dignity of work and contribution, for rich and poor, we have extant to today. Perhaps the concept derived from an old English proverb, "An idle mind is the devil's workshop."[2]

---

2   "Moral Therapy and the Problem of Morale," *The American Journal of Psychiatry* 134, no. 3 (1977), https://doi.org/10.1176/ajp.134.3.267.

By the twentieth century, McLean was where the VIPs went. It was a bit like a country club for mental patients—for the "elite" patient, typically white and rich; there was a tennis court and a (short) golf course. It helped, not just financially, to have celebrity and wealthy patients to provide an aura, a special place where special people like poets, writers, entertainers, and the scions of industry and banking went. After all, a jacket sold on Fifth Avenue will go for more money than the same one on the Lower East Side. By the twentieth century, McLean was the Fifth Avenue of psychiatric services. It became a magnet that attracted accomplished doctors and scientists as its faculty, and those training in psychiatry.

The more the hospital treated VIPs, the stronger became the magnet. By the mid-twentieth century, McLean was regarded as one of the best psychiatric centers in the US, and soon, thereafter, in the world. Revenue and professional recruitment "followed the money," until the end of the twentieth century, when McLean fell on hard times.

I was a bit unglued by disbelief upon my arrival—I was to be McLean's new medical director (though the title was different back then). Title aside, there also was the mystique, the aura, the damn fame of the place.

Yet, I knew from its new president, Dr. Steven Mirin, who had hired me, that the hospital was entering a financial black hole. No one, no place, is immune to the devastation that losing money can bring.

I drove to the hill's peak, set like an eagle's nest atop the 246-acre property. There stood the Administration Building, three floors with a mellow yellow brick exterior, though not so mellow in its interior because hospital admissions were received on its first floor. Wide, granite steps led up to the entrance of the building, flanked by two tall poles proudly displaying the flags of the United States and the Commonwealth of Massachusetts.

I hadn't been assigned a parking space in the front oval of the building; there weren't many and those were rationed to big(ger) shots, visitors, and people with disabilities, who needed more proximate access to the clinical services than the rather distant parking lots afforded. I parked in my given space behind the building, a perk, which did save time. My time, finite as it was, would be swamped. I would be there early every day and liked to work late, being among the last to leave, if you didn't count those who staffed the hospital at night.

I was at the *landing zone*, like arriving at Mars, but with a sizable asteroid headed its way—an asteroid created by the collision of traditional medicine with a new era of the corporatization of American medicine.

THE TERRAIN

In the winter of 1989, I had been working at Mount Auburn Hospital in Cambridge, Massachusetts, and teaching at Cambridge Hospital, another academic site of Harvard Medical School. I had made an appointment to meet with my department chairman. When we met, I said to him, "It's time for me to leave, to move on." I was his associate chief of psychiatry and had acquitted myself in this work, but I was restless (*spilches* in Yiddish), though I had no position to move to.

But only a week or two later, I had a phone call from Steve Mirin, a colleague. He had been a past (unpaid) president of the Massachusetts Psychiatric Society (MPS) a couple of years earlier, and I had just been elected by the society's membership (approximately 1,800 doctors at the time) to serve as its president (also unpaid). But Mirin wasn't calling about the MPS. He knew I had spent the past thirteen years providing general hospital psychiatric services, including inpatient services. Steve asked if I might be interested in doing some consulting for him at McLean Hospital.

Mirin had been recruited back to McLean Hospital to be its medical director, after a successful seven years directing a private psychiatric hospital not far from Boston. He was no stranger to McLean, having previously led services and conducted research at the hospital. His was not a prodigal son story. He was responding to two fire alarms that signaled the imminent peril, perhaps demise, of this 180-year, storied hospital (at the time).

The first alarm was that Shervert Frazier, MD, psychiatrist in chief of McLean—a Texan and legendary figure at McLean and the nationally renowned former head of the NIMH (the National Institute of Mental Health)—was immediately stepping down from his position. Frazier had recruited Mirin back to McLean, knowing that the place needed an overhaul, not just a new coat of paint. But suddenly and unexpectedly, Frazier resigned.

The dean of Harvard Medical School, where Frazier was a professor and chief of a Harvard hospital, had evidence from detailed material he had received that some of Dr. Frazier's professional publications were "plagiarized," a serious violation of professional ethics in any academic setting, no less Harvard. Frazier did not contest the dean's allegations, which, in my view, were minor and unintended. Yet, it was plagiarism to cut and paste (without permission) material from any articles previously published, which he had evidently done, or allowed to happen. He fell on his sword.

When Mirin arrived back at McLean, Frazier asked him to shadow him, which lasted five weeks. That quite brief walk-through became Mirin's preparation to succeed Frazier as psychiatrist in chief, pending board approval. Almost overnight, McLean was thrown into the turmoil of the hospital losing its long-standing and beloved leader, when few thought "the punishment fit the crime." Mirin would become chief and move into Frazier's corner office in the yellow brick Administration Building, designed by William H. McLean and Albert Hoffman Wright. They worked as partners as the hospital moved to its Belmont location in the late nineteenth century.

The second and even greater fire, though not quite ablaze right off, was what would be the breathtaking spread of what we now not so affectionately call "managed care." Like a kudzu plant, it began strangling the roots of naturally occurring hospital life-forms anywhere within its reach. In a managed care organization (MCO), clinical decisions are taken from doctors and hospitals and *owned and determined* by for-profit corporations contracted to control the escalating cost of hospitals and other medical enterprises. McLean, by the way, is a not-for-profit hospital.

While managed care had sprouted in other states, it did not land in Massachusetts until the late 1980s. By all institutional standards, however, this was no evolution in care but rather a type of abrupt coup. It would change the values and operations of American medicine, and McLean was to be no exception. Frazier (and the leadership of the McLean board) surely saw this coming when he decided to hire Mirin.

Clinical decisions were becoming financially driven, under the control of for-profit intermediaries, MCOs, who saved money for their clients by cutting payments to "providers." Mental health and addiction services were especially in their crosshairs because mental and behavioral clinical approvals for care (payment) were harder to prove than the lab and imaging results general medicine could produce, along with ages of stigma about these conditions.

MCOs *guaranteed* cost reductions to their "customers," large insurance companies, a great many, also large, self-insured corporations, and state government agencies. MCOs hold three commanding grips around the necks of medical services.

First, they decide which hospitals and clinicians can be in their "network," which MCOs term preferred providers, namely the hospital systems *they* select and contract with to deliver clinical services. Not being in an MCO network means either not getting approval (read payment) for *any* services provided, or that patients and families need to shoulder substantially higher copayments, or the full freight of an episode of illness. Even prosperous patients and families no longer could afford to pay out of pocket for non-network "providers" for all but the briefest care.

Second, they use their network contracts with hospitals to set per diem (daily) payments for care. MCOs decreased payments by 20 to 40 percent, in some cases, even more. For some hospitals (like McLean), the per diems offered by MCOs for admission and continued care were far from meeting the hospital's *actual cost* per day of operating a bed or service. Paradoxically, volume would only make financial matters worse.

Third, these fiscal and administrative intermediaries installed several burdensome systems that often inhibit or deter the delivery of patient care, including "prior approval" and "concurrent review." Prior approval is when a network doctor or hospital must call some distant 800 number and beseech approval for clinical care from a nonmedical clerk operating off a corporate, computerized, decision-making program (algorithm). Determinations of "not approved" servicers *or* doling out but a few days of coverage at a time were their means of saving money—off of payments to doctors and hospitals, for which MCOs profited. They took significant amounts of money out of patient care. The "approval" (or appeal) process was a painful waste of time, since MCO computer programs must have been written by those in the gambling industry, where the "house" always wins. Decisions made by artificial intelligence (AI), increasingly so, deterred many from making the effort. With concurrent review, the provider clinically responsible for a patient had to go hat in hand *again* and speak with yet another unknown, nonmedical person or a machine at the end of the 800 line to gain approval for payment for a further dollop of services. Sometimes approvals were for one inpatient day at a time.

Corporate-run healthcare was controlling medical services, a change that stood to eradicate their control by medical professionals. MCOs, the fiscal tentacles of large insurers, and state governments made it so McLean could not escape their grip: When McLean was not in an MCO network of hospitals, this meant that McLean received no referrals, limiting the influx of new patients. When McLean was in the network, it meant that McLean received far lower payment for a day of care. The hospital would lose money every day on every patient. Grinding fiscally rather than clinically driven approval processes for admission and continued care were designed to be "just say no" to what could be life-saving treatment—because the MCO was not going to spend more money than it promised to their customers, which was less, never more. And a clerk creating a company debit (not credit) could be placing their job, never publicly stated, in jeopardy. These policies would fill the wallets of MCOs but leave institutions like McLean holding an empty bag, again, because with for-profit companies the "house always wins"—a must-win for the CEO to keep their job. Yet McLean continued to accept a big caseload of quite ill patients, the managed care craziness notwithstanding. MCOs soon became hated not just by doctors and hospitals, but by patients and their families as well. Their power was undeniable—and seemed impossible to resist.

For McLean, not joining MCO networks to avoid their corporate for-profit mission meant the hospital would die a death from empty beds. Joining an MCO network was a different form of death, not only by a thousand paper cuts from seeking endless, *impersonal*, nonmedical approvals, but also by having to agree to "fire sale" payments. This could prove unsustainable and result in institutional death—the slow death of a treasury plagued to drain.

McLean was a very desirable target for the growing MCO movement because it represented traditional medicine with expert, Harvard faculty doctors making decisions. Taking on and taking down McLean could be seen as fatally shooting a big, prized elephant in the herd. And an unwillingness to change by many McLean senior doctors made the place even more of a trophy worth winning.

No organization, like MGH, was going to step in and cover losses—and McLean had no endowment. McLean was going to have to endure years of losses on its financial bottom line—and *by intent* not take the losses out of staffing numbers and pay rates: doing so would likely add quality and safety problems to the fires set when the asteroid hit McLean.

I was not naïve to the corporatization of medicine, but I had *no idea* the extent by which healthcare dollars and services were being diverted from patient care and amassed by investor-owned, for-profit corporations (and privatized public programs).[3]

McLean was not a canary in the coal mine. It was more like Salomon Brothers, then one of the largest and most prominent investment banks in the US, whose chairman/CEO carried the moniker "the King of Wall Street." With its long history of care, its

3   Milton Friedman, "A Friedman Doctrine: The Social Responsibility of Business Is to Increase Its Profits," *New York Times Magazine*, September 13, 1970.

status as Harvard's only psychiatric hospital, and its patient roster of the rich and famous, McLean seemed "too big to fail." But this proved to be a fiction, from the time the asteroid hit.

For eleven years, I was in the center of the hospital's financial and clinical upheaval, when corporatization collided with traditional (and, in some instances, dated) medicine. I can, thus, report firsthand how McLean, with its prominence as an historic Harvard hospital, appeared too big and too important to people of influence and wealth to fail, and yet it almost did.

THE FIRST STEP

Upon entering the side door to the Administrative Building on my first day at McLean, I turned right and proceeded down the first-floor corridor, with but a handful of offices, including mine. The Admin Building also housed, on the first floor as well, two wood-paneled conference rooms that rivaled, in their sober but elegant ambiance, those of any Ivy League university or white-glove law firm. My office was the second on the right, with a lovely cloth bench outside its door. I had never been in, no less seen, my new office. But there, on the door, was a tasteful brass plate with my name and title on it. That felt unreal.

I went into my office, turned on the lights and the already installed desktop computer, and set about to learn the pieces of the McLean puzzle.

2

THE LANDSCAPE AHEAD

McLean, near to 200 years old, does not look its age, not from a distance, looking at its spacious campus on the 246 acres that Frederick Law Olmsted and Calvert Vaux designed with its forty-six buildings, some new, some old but with charm. Decades of financial prosperity and McLean's grand station in the country's mental health and addiction community had lulled too many on the senior professional staff, faculty, and private attendings to thinking all was well, maybe better than ever.

BACKGROUND

On August 11, 1988, Dr. Shervert Frazier, the beloved McLean psychiatrist in chief, left his five-week-old medical director to take up the reins. By October 1988, the McLean board voted to finalize Dr. Steven Mirin's appointment as psychiatrist in chief. He previously had done clinical and research work at McLean and then successfully ran a nearby private, for-profit psychiatric hospital. Mirin had chutzpah and drive. He would serve as McLean's general director and psychiatrist in chief until 1997, when he left to be president of the American Psychiatric Association in Washington, DC.

Few knew in 1989—including many of the hospital's professional staff—that an abundant collection of ideological, operational, and financial problems was eating through a façade of prosperity and invincibility. Conditions that were more than enough to doom any hospital subject to the merciless new era of corporate medicine.

I arrived at McLean in 1989, as it crossed the Rubicon into the Valley of Death. At the outset, it was hard to perceive the nascent clinical and financial free fall to come, but not for long.

Fiscal year 1989 was my baseline for data. McLean was operating 327 inpatient beds, with an average, daily occupancy of 300 patients. The average length of an inpatient stay (ALOS) was over sixty days.

By design, as we reduced the average stay to fifty-seven days, which may seem small, that resulted in a reduction of 2,500 bed days from the previous year. Bed days are a simple calculus: like in a hotel, every unoccupied hotel room is financially analogous to an empty hospital bed, both being their principal, respective revenue streams. McLean, as a Harvard hospital, provided psychiatric training and research but at a financial loss, which was subsidized by revenues from its clinical services. Big trouble lay ahead as clinical revenues diminished.

In 1989, McLean had 1,888 admissions, by no means bountiful from 300 operating beds, which helped fuel the criticism that it was harder to get into McLean Hospital than into Harvard College.

The average daily costs to operate a McLean inpatient bed were considerably greater than for Massachusetts General Hospital's psychiatric unit and vastly greater than the other Boston-area general and private psychiatric hospitals.

But within a year, in 1990, revenues began to fall commensurate with the fall in occupied inpatient beds. The hospital's principal source of revenue was exsanguinating. There was no tourniquet to stem the hemorrhaging of money, which began in 1992 and lasted near to six long years, like dog years.

THE BOOM IN PSYCHIATRIC MEDICATIONS

At its core, the clinical services at McLean at that time held to a well-established and—so far—successful ideology that long-term, psychoanalytically oriented psychotherapy produced change. Yet clinically therapeutic, beneficial change could be achieved by a model of acute, short-term psychiatric services and medications— the greatest innovations in the field, which had been growing in dominance since the 1960s. These medications included lithium for manic-depressive illness—now called bipolar disorder. Lithium was a miracle drug, despite troubling adverse effects on the kidneys, and it was followed by mood stabilizers of all stripes. First-generation antidepressants, replete with side effects and the risk of death from overdose, were then eclipsed by selective serotonin reuptake inhibitors (SSRIs) like fluoxetine (Prozac), sertraline (Zoloft), citalopram (Celexa), and paroxetine (Paxil), as well as serotonin-norepinephrine reuptake inhibitors (SNRIs) like duloxetine (Cymbalta), venlafaxine (Effexor), and the "atypical" bupropion (Wellbutrin). These antidepressant medications are used by 13 percent of the entire US population (twelve years and older).[4] Antipsychotics are used for schizophrenia, schizoaffective disorder (schizophrenia with mood symptoms), bipolar

---

4   Debra J. Brody and Qiuping Gu, "Antidepressant Use among Adults: United States, 2015–2018," *NCHS Data Brief*, no. 377 (September 2020), https://www.cdc.gov/nchs/data/databriefs/db377-H.pdf.

disorder, and borderline and other impulse disorders; they help control acute symptoms like agitation, paranoia, and impulsivity. They held the promise of ending two centuries of institutional care. This promise, however, has gone unfulfilled, considering today's "transinstitutionalism" with jails, prisons, and the streets the default solutions for people acutely and chronically ill with serious and persistent mental disorders. There were also countless tranquilizers, hypnotics, and psychostimulants (amphetamines) in use.

This unprecedented explosion in psychiatric treatments had spread widely in psychiatric and general medical care. But in 1989 it had yet to unseat the ideology at McLean that had existed since the 1950s. Ironically, some of the top experts in psychopharmacology were senior researchers at McLean.

WHAT NEEDED FIXING AND HOW

McLean's clinical practices still hewed to a belief, especially among the hospital's senior, private attending staff, that the proper treatment for mental disorders was psychoanalytic psychotherapy. When delivered to inpatients, that meant long stays in the hospital. The length of stay for a McLean admission could range from a month to a year, a metric that shouted out to corporate healthcare, "Shoot me!"

The provision of long-term, inpatient psychotherapy was a truly dated model of care, which, not incidentally, called for a "T-A (therapist–administrator) split." The patient had one (junior) McLean doctor on the ward—the administrator—who wrote orders, prescribed medications, responded to all crises, worked with the nursing staff, and planned and executed discharge.

The patient also had a therapist, but not on the ward. Instead, this was a member of the hospital's attending staff, private psy-chiatrists and psychologists mostly having no-rent offices on the campus. They separately billed the patient (usually the patient's insurance) and cherry-picked those who could pay. Attendings did not prescribe medications, write orders, or respond to nursing requests. They came to the ward of the patient usually three to four times a week for the proverbial "fifty-minute hour." I could not understand how a patient or family—not to mention a hospital service chief—could discern which doctor was clinically responsi-ble for the patient.

Changing this model of care would not be simple or easy. It would take a set of overlapping and substantial actions to do so, and it would take time. The model that needed to replace long-term inpatient treatment was not unfamiliar to me. I had successfully employed it in three general hospital inpatient units (MGH, Mount Auburn, and Cambridge Hospital)—it was why Mirin wanted me on board. Moreover, I had written *Inpatient Psychiatry: Diagnosis and Treatment* (through three editions), a prominent text used by many residency programs throughout the country. Diverse colleagues a bit younger than me still come up and tell me that my book was foundational and instrumental to their early residency training. Warms an author's heart.

A short-term model for inpatient psychiatry focused on sta-bilizing patients with acute, often suicidal, illnesses. Analytic psychotherapy for patients in severe states of psychotic and depressive illnesses threatens to open a Pandora's box, flooding and destabilizing their acute and fragile mental functioning. A focus on understanding and altering the "focal problem," the events in a person's life that had precipitated their acute illness, was the work that needed to be done. Prompt and prudent use of medications aided in the restoration of functioning, leading to safe discharge to community-based services and supportive families (when present). These ideas, needless to say, were expressed in the hundreds of pages in *Inpatient Psychiatry* and updated in its second and third editions.

MONEY TALKS

Also bearing down on McLean, making it aversive to payers, were its costs. An inpatient day (virtually the entirety of the hospital's clinical revenues) was a distant star on a scattergram of comparable services in the area. Charges per day would reach and extend beyond $1,000, while MCOs were looking to pay $500, maybe $600 daily—in other words, too disparate for negotiation.

McLean's "payers" were a collection of commercial insurers.

McLean was an IMD—an institution for mental disease, defined by federal statute as "a hospital, nursing facility, or other institution of more than sixteen beds that is primarily engaged in providing diagnosis, treatment, or care of persons with mental diseases, including medical attention, nursing care, and related services."[5] Enacted as a section of the Social Security Act of 1972, an IMD is excluded from Medicaid payment for any patient between twenty-one and sixty-five years of age. The IMD exclusion remains today, but most states have skirted it by placing Medicaid under managed care intermediaries. The growth of Medicaid payment at McLean would reach 13 percent by 1993, with Medicaid per diem payments still below McLean's costs. Unless costs were reduced, any growth in the hospital's Medicaid patients would further eat away at revenue.

---

5   "Compilation of the Social Security Laws: Definitions," Social Security Administration, https://www.ssa.gov/OP_Home/ssact/title19/1905.htm.

But it was the calculus of charges per day times the number of days that also sent a loud message to payers: McLean was too expensive and needed to be avoided. Two things had to happen to bring McLean back into the game. First, we needed to reduce its costs per day. Second, we needed to reduce the hospital's average length of stay from sixty-three days when I landed there to fourteen days. Imagine, $1,000 a day for sixty-three days; that's $63,000, while $600 a day for fourteen days is but $8,400. McLean could cost eight times as much as an MCO facility! As they say in Brooklyn, "fuhgeddaboudit."

But that would not suffice because *an organization cannot exit a financial crisis by cost-cutting alone.* A future for McLean would require building new services, diversification, opening the hospital to all strata of diverse patients, and remaking a McLean that our professional community would feel to be receptive, respectful, responsive, and flexible. Nothing less would do.

SETTING THE TABLE

The Yiddish word *ungapatchka* may also help to put the McLean mess in perspective. *Ungapatchka* is an adjective or noun that is not quite complimentary, but is used kindly, forgivingly, and always with a dollop of humor. Its use is broad, including for a place, person, meal, big idea, report, even a book! An *ungapatchka* place is a bit chaotic, doing senseless, unnecessary, and excessive things, decked out but with too much junk. But it is implicitly salvageable because it involves good people trying to do good. They may simply be lost as to how to escape their disorganization and tumult.

The first thing you might want to do upon entering an unga-patchked home is to start putting things where they ought to be, like books on shelves rather than as obstacles on the floor to hurdle, moving the pots and pans out of the clothes closet into the kitchen, the TV made visible from the couch and chairs, fixing a pantry so it would not do you damage when its overly stuffed goods fall onto your head.

3

THE BEST OF INTENTIONS

You've heard, I imagine, the proverb "The road to hell is paved with good intentions." I prefer a lesser-known (and different) variation that "hell is full of good meanings, but heaven is full of good works" because what truly counts is results, not intentions.

Good intentions—meaning well—that lead to hell may be genuine, misinformed, disinformed (a popular term post-2017), or the expression of self-interest wrapped to appear as for the greater good. There surely are blends of these varied states of human behavior.

These motivational variants can dispose observers to different feelings and judgments by those who harbor them, like empathy and kindness, naïve gratitude, forgiveness, disdain, and anger. The imperative, whatever the motivation, is to give good intentions a quick burial, lest you be swept up in their path to hell.

THE HOSPITAL'S CAST
OF PRIVATE DOCTORS

Set a bit away from the central campus buildings, on a rise in McLean's topography, was an old brick building, Higginson House. While I was seldom there, I could see it from a variety of locations on McLean's grounds. Some time ago, well before I began at McLean, the building had been given over to the hospital's private practice attendings, psychiatrists and psychologists. There were a lot of offices at Higginson House, since every floor had rows of offices, and it had quite a few floors. There was a small parking lot in front—I hoped, for patients.

The Higginson professional staff did not directly or significantly contribute to McLean revenues. But they were instrumental to its culture. They had been the bearers of McLean's belief in long-term hospitalization and treatment that was psychoanalytically focused. Neither a long-term nor analytic approach had a body of supporting professional evidence, especially for severe and chronic mental illness. Higginson's influence on McLean's clinical culture (and practice) of long-term psychanalytic psychotherapy was a big problem for the team in the Admin Building: because that treatment was antithetical to the model of *acute* psychiatric care, which we considered essential to keeping McLean alive.

The attendings were amassed in Higginson House, on the McLean campus, placing them in the geographic center of the hospital; they were inescapable in their presence and their influence. They had been dominant as an element in the well water that had nourished McLean's clinical services but now were antithetical to our mission to make McLean sustainable, for it to be medically in the modern world. To save the hospital, we had to do battle with the best intentions that we knew occupied the road to McLean's demise. By no means did we need to face the predominance of

Higginson House's occupants. But as it would take a small group of "committed citizens" to right the hospital, so it could take a small group of well-meaning but clueless "citizens" (at Higginson House) to be its detriment. We were trying to save McLean for a future of effective and needed patient care, not for the attendings— nor could we, in any case.

Attendings were psychiatrists and psychologists in private practice. They held appointments at the distinguished Harvard Medical School (HMS), with academic titles granted to them by virtue of their being "voluntary" McLean professional staff. This meant contributing a few hours per week of their time to supervise trainees or teach or—as it turned out—to cover clinical services when the residents were in their "protected time" of classes and seminars. Protected time was inviolate at academic centers, like McLean. But patient care did not, could not, stop. We needed doctors to cover for doctors (residents), previously unheard of and resisted. But those attendings who wanted to continue their Harvard appointment and practice out of a (private) McLean office got the message: they were needed for patient care, first and foremost.

The attendings were not on the payroll of the hospital. They privately billed their patients, whom they saw on the hospital's inpatient units, in McLean's on-campus residences, and as outpatients in their on-campus offices, or sometimes in nearby offices off the grounds of the hospital.

There was no winning over a small number of established, senior, and influential McLean doctors who thought they knew what could save McLean. They asserted that the Mirin team was "ruining" the hospital.

We wanted a different McLean, which would deliver not only acute care, but also serve people living in or near poverty, many of whom were people of color. These were a large group of potential patients for whom private doctor fees were prohibitively low or to whom insurers paid paltry fees, well below the "water level" the attendings were accustomed to.

Though not publicly stated, there was yet another source of enmity. We (Mirin and company) had passed over some of these doctors in our selections of leaders for McLean's growing clinical services. Some had to have imagined they were in line for advancement to a leadership position. After all, they had been there for many years and worked diligently to climb the professional (not academic or research) ladder. I imagine some may have thought that the Harvard imprimatur made the hospital—and, by extension, them—invincible. Even then, and for many years earlier in my career, I knew otherwise. Academic institutions, especially those who top the charts, are not charitable to their faculty and employees. Cloistered and sheltered from the storm for many years left many McLean senior doctors with too little experience, hence little appreciation, of the world outside the gates of McLean Hospital.

I believed their intentions were to sustain a booming McLean, while in fact no such possibility continued to exist. It's different when a group's intentions are not well-meaning; then, it's acceptable to confront the enemy at the gates of McLean Hospital, more acceptable to publicly make your case. But do-gooders who think their cause is just and necessary are no less dangerous than palpable foes because they can reach the heart of the many others needed to save McLean.

FIELDWORK

In my new job, I knew to make the rounds to visit the senior doctors, by appointment, in their office, not mine. I appreciated that some had been "passed over," "benched," making them important to see, to not add the insult of neglect to their likely felt injury. None of this group were going to abide by our emerging plans, no less accept or help with the path that Mirin (me and others) had chosen. But my aim was not to try to persuade them or win them over—that would be naïve and wasteful of precious time. I also knew that it could be painful and disorienting to be out in the professional cold after you had labored long and hard. I knew that personally.

I became a target of their disappointment and anger. It's part of the human condition to seek to blame someone else for your fall from grace. Psychiatrists (like me) are students of the human nature that abounds, and ought to see things as they are, best so when not about their self. I went to see a senior psychiatrist who had been a candidate for leading a clinical program. He sat at his rather empty, big old oak desk, squarely facing me. He said I would fail, that I would be out of McLean in disgrace in short order, too. I said nothing in response. It was a brief meeting.

Later that day, I told this tale to my often-bemused boss, Steven Mirin, who smiled and sent me back to work. We did not fail. We were the winning team, but it took a long time to succeed. This angry doctor soon found his way to another hospital. His leaving was no victory for me or the McLean executive team, just another step forward for McLean, which would benefit from less opposition and disdain from members of its senior staff. These were doctors looking in the rearview mirror. They were going to miss the chance to continue at McLean by helping to save it so it could be, would be, once again, one of the finest psychiatric hospitals in the world.

The McLean attendings, on campus and off, brought in very few hospital admissions, as once did the attending medical staff in general hospitals for medical and surgical intensive care. Instead, the McLean attendings were part of the McLean tradition of delivering psychoanalytically oriented therapy to patients admitted by others in our professional community.

With inpatients, they delivered on the model of care they espoused and promoted. They still believed they were doing the right thing, with the best of intentions regarding what was best for the patient, even when that was no longer the case. Their influence continued to prevail throughout this iconic hospital, which was about to be blasted by the asteroid of corporate medicine.

Central to their model of treatment, sometimes daily, or a few times a week, the attendings would put in their fifty-minute therapy hour on the wards (or elsewhere on campus), and then be gone. To my amazement, the attendings generally did not prescribe medications for McLean hospital patients, who were quite ill and needing hospitalization, as well as good psychopharmacological treatment. That was left to the "junior" psychiatric hospital staff, starting off their careers—as a rule. They were the unit PICs (psychiatrists in charge). The PICs had to call and persuade the attendings to provide therapy for patients on the ward—a tough sell when payment for private fees was becoming no longer ample. The PICs received low pay rates: I recall it was about $40,000 a year.

BETWEEN A (CLINICAL) ROCK
AND A (FINANCIAL) HARD PLACE

Early on, making the rounds on an inpatient unit, I ran into one of the exceptional PICs we had at McLean. She was rushing through discussing her orders with the nursing staff. She seemed pleased to see me but could not stop to talk. She needed to finish on the ward as soon as possible and head to her private office in nearby downtown Belmont. One result of the low pay we paid PICs was they had to earn more money to support themselves, their families, a mortgage, and very often hefty student loans that followed them like dark clouds. The hospital was not financially giving her what she needed to allow for more time with her inpatients, their families, nursing staff, and colleagues. The consequences of the "best of (prevailing) intentions" had landed on her shore, and that of other PICs, as if their burden was not great enough.

While many PICs were reconciled to this arrangement as their "dues," the tolls on the bridge to greater seniority and a more robust private practice, the hospital was effectively putting the PICs between a (clinical) rock and a (financial) hard place. This was not a formula to achieve the best of patient care, especially briefer, more acute care, which was to be the new clinical mission of McLean. The PIC financial short-sheeting had to change—another item added to the long, growing list of to-dos.

A great many attendings stayed the course during the years of upheaval in saving McLean. Some took hospital paid positions when we created a staff model of care, which was very different from an attending model; the staff doctors are employed by the hospital, which is common today in medicine, where hospital-based and paid inpatient doctors often are called "hospitalists."

Many attendings were still at McLean five or six years later to see us surface from the cold sea of change and breathe in the oxygen of the future. Many stayed on for years. Traditions have their benefits, not just limitations. These were the doctors whose intentions aligned with saving the hospital.

FREE OFFICES?

To my amazement, as I mentioned earlier, the attendings paid no rent to use their offices. Their offices were McLean Hospital *property*, with their full costs borne by the hospital. Yet these professional staff were not helping to staunch the hospital's hemorrhaging money. Prone sometimes to judgment, I could comprehend their hesitancy to join in keeping McLean from going under, and I could not brook it. We needed players, not spectators; givers, not takers; donors, not recipients. What we needed least of all were icy stares and verbal critique. We especially needed help covering the Admissions Unit the few hours each week when the residents were in seminars. We needed clinical help with the increasingly robust flow of admissions, as well as with other clinical service needs. But that was not what we were getting, with some exceptions.

Then, as if the clouds parted, we had a solution, one we did not initiate but actually had no choice but to capitalize on. Our keen chief financial officer, David LaGasse, announced "we have a problem" at an executive team meeting. He had learned that the provision of "free" offices to doctors on the staff of hospitals (and other healthcare settings) would likely be interpreted by federal regulatory agencies as what is called "inurement."

Even the appearance of inurement was anathema; McLean was going to do what was right and that was how our practices would be seen. Providing free offices could well appear as a kickback for the presumed referrals they made to the hospital, even if that was not the case. We had enough to do without answering to a federal audit, with liability for federal financial punishments and nightmarish regulatory demands—for our giving free offices to attendings. By the way, free offices also were not what you wanted to appear in a national newspaper, as it might. Iconic settings are usually not local news; they draw an audience from coast to coast.

Not abiding by the federal regulations that were strapped all around Medicare and Medicaid (with their massive enrollment and McLean's growing population of patients on entitlement programs) was a bad thing to be doing. We wanted to continue, and increase, our care of people in these entitlement programs because that would be a significant step in achieving social and racial equity. We also wanted to grow our clinical care revenues— but not if there was a threat of damaging McLean's lifeline to already shrinking revenues. To a federal regulator, it would make no sense to provide doctors with free offices (inurement), unless that practice was seen as a means to swell hospital admissions and days. Not incidentally, more admissions meant greater costs for these federal agencies to bear. McLean leadership was not keen on being viewed as engaging in any form of legerdemain that might fleece the federal government. Indeed, what we were doing was no different from a bribe, except we got nothing from many of the flock of attendings gathered in Higginson House. At stake were swift and harsh federal financial punishments. Mind you, a very small number of admissions could be attributed to the attendings. But no matter, in what often can be seen as a black-and-white situation. Ironically, McLean's well-meaning practice of providing doctors free offices could land us in a well-meaning hell.

There would be no shelter from a charge of inurement, which we could contest. But fighting with the federal (or state or city) government was a fool's errand, a black hole of time and money. As my parents taught me, "Don't fight city hall." The burden of a legal case going on for years, as these do, would mean losing every step of the way, *even* if we won. Federal rule violations are best avoided, which we could (and did) do, allowing for some time to change to rental agreements in Higginson House, and, thus, return to "compliance" with the feds.

We prepared to meet with the attendings, represented by their leadership. That was not going to be a walk in the (McLean) park. Our CFO and COO had determined and documented a

range of comparable office rental costs in the area. Our inurement problem was not about office space; it was that the office
space was given away by the hospital, free of charge. Meaning we
would not have to take on any battle about allocating space, one
of the most precious commodities in a hospital, but rather who
paid for it, or not.

We had calculated a range of fair market rents, principally
determined by office square footage. We offered the attendings
defensible, lower range rental fees to accommodate all attendings,
some of whom made important academic contributions. Whatever we did also needed to minimize disruptions in patient care.
We were already in peril to close or be bought, so it was best not to
show clinical problems on top of financial ones.

All very rational—but we were not exactly expecting reasoning
to prevail, at least initially. More likely, many Higginson House
attendings could see rental charges, never before done, as retribution or greed, rather than legal protection for all of us.

While this rental arrangement would take time to implement
(money and space do take time to manage), we had decided (and
documented) the prompt and proper action needed to respond
in the event of any federal allegation of inurement. Some of the
attendings moved out. Most stayed. We got through it, but if
Mirin and others on our administrative team already had a short
list of friends, it had grown shorter.

The attending psychiatrists and psychologists had no motives to
milk McLean of its supposed riches. It was not money that fueled
their resistance to change. Many carried within them a rather
unshakable view that their well-intended way, intensive, long-term
psychotherapy, was the best model of care needed for the hospital
to thrive once again. But it was not, and nothing was going to
stop us from building an acute care hospital for psychiatric and

addiction disorders, with a range of services within each. That was what would save McLean (as it did).

I believe that the attendings had no ill intent. They wanted what they thought was a model of psychiatric care that was of the past, not the present; I suppose they didn't get the memo. Theirs was not, to their thinking, a path intended to lead to the demise of McLean Hospital. But the asteroid carrying the corporatization of American medicine had hit Earth. The corporatization of American medicine, including psychiatry, knew few exceptions. McLean Hospital was no exemption. Corporate healthcare was designed, first and foremost, to make a profit, no matter what.

Still, the Mirin leadership team had to face and overcome resistance to our plan for radical change. There were clinical staff at McLean, people of reputation and integrity, with the best of intentions: Many still believed McLean was doing very well and that the clinical changes underway would destroy its quality and reputation. Their resistance and publicly damaging statements were well-meaning, as they must have thought they could revive a dying beast. Many felt that Team Mirin, with Sederer as a point guard, would irreparably ruin a fine hospital, one that had achieved "four stars" over a very long career. But achievement medals are transitory, with new ones meant to be won.

4

FAMILIES

Families—sometimes you can't live with them. But as a rule, it's much more difficult to live without them. For people with a serious and chronic disease, family is often the most enduring of supports. Diseases such as obstructive airway disease, type 1 diabetes, cancer, rheumatoid arthritis, lupus, and mental disorders like schizophrenia, schizoaffective disorder, bipolar illness, major depression, PTSD, and of course the addictions.

A supportive family is the antidote to feeling alone; loneliness has the same deleterious effect on our bodies as does smoking fifteen cigarettes a day.[6] Other supports from family include housing, transportation, money, and hope, to name a few. Family and close friends are the prescription for the adage "don't go it alone."

---

6   Vivek H. Murthy, MD, "Our Epidemic of Loneliness and Isolation: The US Surgeon General's Advisory on the Healing Effects of Social Connection and Community," (2023), 4, www.hhs.gov.

Theories proffering the nature of family dynamics date back to the 1950s (its predecessor was marital counseling). A pioneer was Murray Bowen, MD, a psychiatrist. Bowen did not center his studies on mental illness. His work was about the dynamics and emotional demands of life in a family. He shifted the lens of human development from the individual in a family to the family dynamics and their role in the emotions and development of its members.

Bowen opened the theoretical door to how developmental disorders, including mental illnesses, were the result of disturbances in the family. Enter a host of family dynamic theorists, drawing their roots and guns from wide and far: psychoanalysis (Nathan Ackerman), family systems (Murray Bowen), operant conditioning (Albert Ellis), unclear communications and "double-bind" messages (Gregory Bateson), dysfunction as purposeful in maintaining a family's hierarchy (Jay Haley), existential human encounters (Carl Whitaker), family structure and power (Salvador Minuchin/eating disorders), and many others. Suffice to say that mental disorders were considered a product of family dysfunctions, with the implicit or explicit *blame* that mental disorders were caused by the troubled states of families.

Psychiatry then—and now—has been on a perennial search to explain mental illnesses. Family theory and therapy laid etiology for psychiatry's rather inexplicable mental disorders at the feet of the family. Which did turn needed attention to families, but too much so as the basis for psychopathology. One clear, if inadvertent, result was to make families pariahs in the world of psychiatric treatments. This is antithetical to the good treatment of patients with mental or any medical conditions as a means by which the clinician, patient, and the family can determine whether a treatment is working or not.

WALKING THE WALK

I was in my office at McLean busying myself with paperwork when one of the hospital's program chiefs looked in my open door. You can't win a war with just generals. Majors and captains leading local and widespread campaigns are needed. I invited my colleague in, warmed by the thought that he saw us waging the same battles.

"You're likely to get an angry call from the parents of a psychotically ill patient, over the age of majority," he said. They wanted to see the young man's doctor, who had repeatedly rebuffed their calls. The story I then heard was that this patient was seriously ill with a psychotic illness, with an absence of insight, so he did not believe he was ill (rather, that we were persecuting him). He was refusing medications. He was also dependent on his family for money and a home, so he had no other place to go. But he had exercised his legal rights as a patient to deny visitors, including his family, and, using his "privacy" rights, he foreclosed any hospital communication with any family member. This mess of contradictions is not at all uncommon at a mental hospital. There must have been twenty others in our hospital with a similar profile.

I asked my colleague, the doctor with oversight of this patient's ward, what he thought of my meeting with the parents, with him, the unit doctor, a social worker, and a senior nurse on the ward. As I have revealed elsewhere in this book, I am given to jumping off cliffs. But here, I shimmied up to the edge for two good reasons: one, of course, was assuring the proper care of this patient in the hospital and after discharge, and the other was that I had come to see family excluded too often in the everyday clinical business of McLean. It was a chance early on in my role as medical director to make my position about families known and to contend with yet another cultural problem at the hospital, aggravated by the prevailing regulations of the Health Insurance Portability and Accountability Act of 1996 (HIPAA), which gave health privacy a dominant role in the course of medical care.

We arranged to meet with the young man's parents in a private conference room that was not on the patient's ward. They were grateful, not incensed, that McLean doctors were going to give them insight into their son's condition and find ways they could contribute to his recovery.

When they previously had called, they were told that neither the doctor nor other clinical staff could speak with them because of HIPAA (a new term and concept to them). For families of patients on a psychiatric ward (or in an emergency department), a wall comes up almost immediately that separates patients from families and vice versa. They are customarily told, as an "explanation," that the hospital is abiding by a privacy policy that derives from federal regulations—in this case, HIPAA.

The young man's parents were not angry, as many are when meeting in the wake of their concerns having been dismissed. Expect, as a rule, angry parents, siblings, and other relatives as well, when we doctors act egregiously. We all can learn to not act defensively to angry words; rather, to listen and validate the family's experience of the hospital. Acting effectively with upset people, families, and many others is a skill that can be observed, developed, and used. There are moments to squarely and ably face calcified clinical practices for the sake of all involved.

In a half-hour meeting, we put this young man's treatment—and future—back on the right track. I learned later that he had relented and rescinded his demand that no one in his family was to be allowed to be in contact with McLean staff. I also learned that when he met with his parents later that day—as happens again and again—collectively, they were relieved to be together.

It was the start we sought and accomplished, another building block in the culture change that would be essential to the future of the hospital.

Family exclusion from loved ones is sadly matched by an outdated view: by early family theory work, misinformation, and blame consolidated into the family's portrayal as the *cause* of a loved one's mental disorder. Effective work, over many years, by advocates and families has diminished this damaging and wrong depiction of families. While progress is good, it is not far enough along to fully recognize and respect the role, responsibility, and great asset that families can represent for people with chronic medical conditions over the course of their lifetime.

There is an Irish saying (I paraphrase), when you come to a wall, toss your hat over it and go get it. The HIPAA privacy regulations are not impervious, not a concrete wall. They are porous, in that HIPAA recognizes emergencies and other grave moments in a person's life, and allows for essential communications among patients, doctors, and families. Moreover, I have never, *ever* seen a doctor sued for speaking to a family of a patient, especially when urgent and essential decisions must be made (as it is during psychiatric hospitalization).

Some critics of mental healthcare suggest that doctors "hide behind HIPAA." This would be a means, they think, to elude the type of litigation going on extensively in medical services, a legal "defense" against malpractice litigation for privacy violation. Though, some doctors would add it is to spare themselves what can be demanding work with families. I have no tolerance for avoiding needed clinical communications, and so would the hospital's services I was responsible for.

But HIPAA, in my early years at McLean, cast a shadow over clinical services, not letting the light shine in on essential and urgent clinical conversations. That problem was squarely in my court at McLean.

The culture change needed to put HIPAA in its proper perspective and, more so, to allow for essential hospital communications—in the interests of patients and their families—cannot be achieved by mandates or exhortation, I think. It's better to learn by doing how best to communicate when actively serving the needs of a patient (and their family). If I took a step toward the light, others would more likely dare to follow, even if that required to learn (mostly by example) the skills needed to engage and inform, to seize the moment for the good of your patient and those immediate to that person's life. Making that happen throughout all of McLean, all the time, needed doing. Good communication is a fundamental principle in the life of a hospital. McLean's standing in the professional and lay communities could only benefit if our clinicians acted sensibly, rather than "hiding" behind HIPAA.

I had no way of measuring avoidance of the families of hospitalized patients, but I assumed it was a significant problem because of the lingering bias against families, which had accrued for fifty or more years. Bias too, I have learned, can be overcome by clinically informed, direct, face-to-face experiences among patients, their families, and hospital staff. Honest, respectful, and direct encounters, after all, may be the best medicine my field has in overcoming bias and discrimination.

Some years later in my role as CMO of the largest state mental health agency in the country, the topic of HIPAA privacy came up in my regular meeting with the forty or so psychiatrist leaders of the agency's twenty-two state hospitals. The agency operated (then) well over 3,000 hospital beds and served over 25,000 people, annually, in its outpatient clinics.

By that time, I had already spoken my piece on this matter in a *Wall Street Journal* op-ed:[7] "An individual with a mental illness that interferes with his judgment, self-interest, self-preservation, and safety represents a profound challenge for families and clinicians. Doctors have remarked that when patient rights exceed truly necessary protections, individuals with mental illness can 'die with their rights on.' Sometimes they may harm others along the way."

But that was in a newspaper, albeit one with heft, not a personal exchange with my colleagues, the clinical leaders of New York State's public mental health system. Here too, face to face, if possible, is the best method to use, once again post-COVID.

I've learned to look for moments to respectfully engage with colleagues about the uncertainties and differences that abound in medical care. I hope you take such proverbial bulls by the horns as you exercise your leadership responsibilities. You will be glad you did, as will your colleagues doing the hard work of treating patients and working with their families.

The culture of a hospital clinic, educational facility, service corporation, and many other organizations inescapably includes the families of all those working in all those settings. An organization cannot "hum" and achieve excellence when it avoids and buries the active concerns of patients, students, employees, and the other life-forms who make for the production and services they provide.

Mental (and addictive) disorders are ubiquitous in our societies (over one-fifth of American adults are affected and functionally impaired annually), which means the shadow of illness falls on

---

7   Lloyd Sederer, "The Tragedy of Mental-Health Law: Patient Protections Have Become Rigid Rules Excluding Families from Patient Care and Exceeding Common Sense," *Wall Street Journal*, January 12, 2013.

multiples of those directly impacted by an illness.[8] That's near to seventy million Americans, not a number to ignore or dismiss.[9]

When mental illness enters a family, especially when there is serious and persistent illness, its members are impacted, as well as the person who is ill. You as a clinician, or as an organization, are in a position to transport a family from the experience of "there's nothing they can do" to their being instrumental in the long-term course of their loved one's illness.

Patients with chronic obstructive airway disease often require oxygen. That can be a needed part of good, comprehensive treatment. Not providing them with oxygen will result in their further suffering, a poor course of illness, and risk of death. Families are oxygen in the treatment of mental (and addictive) conditions.

Your organization bears the responsibility of identifying mental illness when an employee's work performance is compromised by an illness. But we know that family functioning during a loved one's illness is also affected. One of a family's greatest challenges is understanding how a loved one with a mental illness, especially when their loved one is acutely ill, may show impaired judgment, singular self-interest, diminished self-care, mood instability, lack of insight, and compromised safety. Often families of people with a serious mental disorder will seek a culprit to explain these profound and worrisome behaviors. Many families turn the mirror on themselves, making it necessary *for you* to convey a central message: It's not their fault. That too, COVID notwithstanding, is always best when face to face, where genuine sentiments usually cannot hide.

---

8   National Institute of Mental Health, https://www.nimh.nih.gov/health/statistics/mental-illness.

9   Congressional Budget Office, https://www.cbo.gov/.

Thus, it's not enough to stay silent with families as they struggle with the mental illness of a loved one. Silence leaves them continuing to find fault with themselves. They need to be spared that conclusion by being told (with the predominance of families) that they are not to blame. You can use these troubled moments to reduce the stress in the family *and* to create an important, long-term advocate for your patient. McLean needed to adopt this culture shift to achieve the caliber of a world-class hospital.

A related and also essential cultural shift for McLean's clinical and administrative staff was to not make things harder for families of a person with a mental or addictive disorder. They already are heartbroken and have a long and hard climb ahead of them. Create and support a culture that lets families know it's not their fault *and* that they can make a helpful difference, whatever that might be. Find and help those families realize their value; help them learn, individually, as well as in small groups, what support feels like. That's how you change their hearts and minds.

PRINCIPLES OF GOOD CARE

As McLean evolved in the early 1990s, so did its *principles of good care*. Principles are not an abstraction unless they're made to be. They are guiding lights in clinical care, how a doctor, nurse, and fellow clinicians best care for their patient. Many principles were in place at McLean, some commonly in practice, and some needed changing.

Several principles stood out as missing throughout the hospital, I thought. One is that treatment should be safe, not traumatic. Another is that treatment should be collaborative, where decisions, small and large, are made with the patient and the patient's family. Inform them about the treatment plan you think best and give them choices. And then go about engaging them in realizing the plan you and they decide upon.

Furthermore, all of us involved in healthcare, doctors, nurses, psychologists, support staff, administrators, and many others need to build a culture, a way of being, in which the patient is an active agent in their own care. When they are, they are much more apt to follow their treatment plan, as well as feel treated with respect and dignity, as you would want for you and your family.

Invite "patient preferences" too if you want to achieve your patient's most effective treatment. This is leaving "traditional medicine behind," but in a good way. It's not that the doctor doesn't know what can make a difference, but rather you as a doctor or other mental health professional owe your patient the opportunity to state their preferences when there are choices for the plan of treatment, which is usually the case.

One good thing is that acting on these principles is *free*. No budget to create and fund. No expenses that cannot be covered. The heart of good medical care is to adopt a recovery-oriented culture. You know it is there when the future is built with what people want—namely purpose, relationships, and contribution—and when you, your colleagues, and the hospital provide what is most important of all: hope.

Yes, I do have a point of view about families and their role in the life of us all, which includes the families of people with mental and addictive disorders. Don't leave any asset unused. The McLean culture would need to consistently voice that families are not a liability. Paradoxically, the best deterrent to malpractice claims is talking with patients and their families: Be kind and helpful, and they will join you in the hard work of recovery. By the way, I learned about who gets sued and who does not as McLean's primary liaison to Harvard's Risk Management Foundation, which self-insures all the Harvard hospitals—and there were many back then and even more today.

My view about families and my mission to maintain a culture that was attuned to them did not come by coincidence. Early on in my career, I spent a year training in families and family therapy in Cambridge, Massachusetts. That training, which I still use frequently, sensitized me to looking beyond the patient (often called the "identified patient") to see a patient's family and other relationships, and appreciating their impact on a patient, or any group of people. You can think of this as reversing the "figure-ground," where the context, the family, becomes the "figure" and the person recedes, becoming a part of the "ground."

Families are not to be avoided: They are the water we all swim in. Without families, we individuals are like beached whales. My thanks and appreciation to the Cambridge Family Institute, and to my teachers over the years educating me about families.

5

HUBRIS

*H*ubris is as old as it is prevalent, almost as if it were as instinctive as sex and aggression. It is derived from an ancient Greek term with roots from the concepts of both honor (τιμή, *timē*) and shame (αιδώς, *aidōs*). This seeming paradox that shame inhabits states of honor can be understood when one person's honor (more like overweening pride) instills shame in another person. This form of hubris takes at least two to tango. Hubris bears a kinship with arrogance. Fervid confidence is often a protective façade that masks deeply felt self-doubts, with their attendant shame.

McLean's curse of prosperity included a full census, waiting lists for admission, the revenue to support a teaching hospital set in Olmsted Park, and a highly competitive position for attracting prominent faculty and top-echelon trainees in psychiatry, psychology, and neuroscience. But by the late 1980s, the hospital's protective veneer offered little defense against inner doubt and the growing invasion of corporate medicine. Denial doesn't work well under these circumstances.

NOSEDIVE

In telegraphic form, here is how the nosedive began. On August 11, 1988 (FY 1988), Dr. Shervert Frazier, the beloved McLean psychiatrist in chief, left peremptorily, leaving his five-week-old medical director to take up the reins. By October 1988, the McLean board voted to finalize Dr. Steven Mirin's appointment as psychiatrist in chief. He was the tip of the spear of McLean's transformation.

In 1989, my data baseline, McLean's "payers" were a collection of insurers. That year, McLean had 1,888 admissions, by no means a bounty from 300 operating beds, which helped fuel the criticism that it was harder to get into McLean Hospital than into Harvard College. The average daily costs to operate an inpatient McLean bed were considerably greater than for Massachusetts General Hospital's psychiatric unit, and vastly greater than the other Boston-area general and private psychiatric hospitals.

McLean's "payers" were a collection of insurers. McLean was an IMD—an institution for mental disease—defined by federal statute as "a hospital, nursing facility, or other institution of more than sixteen beds that is primarily engaged in providing diagnosis, treatment, or care of persons with mental diseases, including medical attention, nursing care, and related services."[10]

Enacted as a section of the Social Security Act of 1972, an IMD is excluded from Medicaid payment for any patient between twenty-one and sixty-five years of age. The IMD regulatory

---

10 "Compilation of the Social Security Laws: Definitions," Social Security Administration, https://www.ssa.gov/OP_Home/ssact/title19/1905.htm.

exclusion remains today, but most states have skirted it by placing Medicaid under managed care intermediaries. The growth of Medicaid payment at McLean would reach 13 percent by 1993, with Medicaid per diem payments well below McLean's costs—making imperative that costs needed to be reduced as patients covered by Medicaid grew in number.

Celebrity added an elite layer to the hospital's façade. The powerful glitter left by past patients like Robert Lowell, Frederick Law Olmsted, Sylvia Plath, John Nash, Ray Charles, and James Taylor was slow to lose its shine. Not many hospitals have a poem written about them by a Nobel laureate or a popular tune. But McLean did. Still, prominence in its reputation was eroding (then the asteroid hit). I was not immune to the hubris of being a doctor to the rich and famous, I must admit, when the opportunity came my way.

None of these celebrities were at McLean during my watch. But if royalty qualifies as celebrity, then there is one story—on my watch—to tell that portrays a hospital that draws the rich and famous *and* was alive with hubris, thinking it could do just about anything. I was instrumental to that hubris.

THE PRINCESS

I was on my way to Logan Airport to meet my new patient, her doctor, and her two "servants." I had arranged for a limousine, a car, and a small van (to carry her bags). She was flying in from the Middle East. As I had learned about VIPs, my presence at the airport was expected, and it even might have had the effect of making her feel welcome. It was wintertime in New England.

Let's call my patient "Princess W"—to confer and protect her station in her country.

I thought, too, that my greeting them upon arrival would make the right impression with the (palace) doctor, since, of course, that was precisely what he would have done. It would also enable me to gather first impressions of the sort that can escape our view once someone arrives at a hospital.

THE BEST OF CARE?

This story is about a woman who was provided what could be considered the "best of psychiatric care," which, nevertheless, proved not good enough. That "best of care," however, is for those who are born and raised in a developed, Western nation and are fluent in English. Which was the profile of the culture and care at McLean Hospital. But there are *billions* of others on this globe for whom culture, language, stigma, and life experiences are quite different, neither good nor bad, but different.

That difference may mean little when receiving specialty medical services—for example, setting a bone fracture, replacing a hip or knee, having lens implantation for cataracts, and bowel surgery for cancer. But that's not so for psychiatric treatment, which eminently relies on language, ethnicity, customs, and an understanding of mental and addiction disorders and their "cures." McLean's specialty psychiatric care could align and distinguish itself with hundreds of millions of people, but far from all.

It is hubris to imagine that a Western psychiatric hospital can rise above any and all of the psychosocial elements a person brings to the therapeutic encounter. Yet, in retrospect, that happened in agreeing to treat Princess W at McLean Hospital. "Goodness of fit" is a valuable term in the practice of psychiatry.

There also is a widespread myth that rich or famous people always get the best of medical care. Of course, those who are poor, marginalized, and stigmatized have a much harder time of it. But wealth (or fame) itself does not ensure the best treatment, or the best of clinical outcomes.

Because, ironically, "special," customized treatment in all medical specialties is prone to greater than usual errors. By definition, "special" deviates from the customary standards of care, as well as routinely reliable procedures. There may be a blind eye to the fundamentals and measures of quality of clinical care in order to please the patient or family. You probably have heard it said that if you need surgery, find someone (at a facility) who does the procedure all the time—because, in effect, practice helps a great deal in achieving perfection. If and when you go for medical care, don't ask to be treated differently; instead, ask to be treated just as well as everyone else.

This tale began about a month earlier than the princess's arrival in Boston. I was in my office after rounding on the hospital's wards. I received a phone message to call a colleague, a physician at Massachusetts General Hospital (MGH). This was unusual. Usually we at McLean, a psychiatric facility, were calling MGH for a variety of medical consults, not the other way around.

In 1819, a state charter simultaneously founded MGH and McLean Hospital. Together, they were to serve the state's citizens in need of medical and (what was then called) asylum care, respectively. Since that time, the two hospitals have been administratively intertwined. Both MGH and McLean became teaching and training hospitals of the Harvard Medical School (HMS).

My MGH colleague told me he had received a call from a doctor in the Middle East who wanted to bring a patient to the US for consultation and treatment. A psychiatric patient who is a "royal." Was McLean interested? Of course, I replied, and I asked him to tell me more.

The MGH doctor continued: He had taken a call from a physician, let's call him "Dr. M," who served as one of the palace doctors. Dr. M indicated that there was a "problem with one of the women," a princess.

Dr. M had arranged for consultation with a psychiatrist in the area. But the patient was not doing well. Moreover, evidently, there had been a few times she had acted "strangely," which he did not elaborate on, except to say that her behavior had been an "embarrassment" to the family. My colleague asked me, "Perhaps you would like to call the doctor there and get more information?" That could not only be helpful to the princess and her family and might also further Harvard's collaboration between medical schools and hospitals in their country. The stakes had just been raised.

My MGH colleague assured me that if McLean accepted Princess W for evaluation and treatment, he would arrange any general medical and neurological consultations she might warrant.

My secretary arranged a call with Dr. M for the next day. I tried to remember what little I knew about her country: its culture, its values, its medical care, and, especially, how mental illness was regarded and treated. I did not know much of that at all, and I was far more in the dark about the world of royal families, no less this one. How might their extraordinary privilege and station in life shape their thinking, their expectations? I wondered.

McLean, radically getting back on track, was arguably one of the finest psychiatric hospitals in the world. McLean, I had wrongly thought then, could effectively serve the princess (and her family). At the same time, I briefly thought and dismissed what I had already seen with other US and international (VIP) patients who had made the psychiatric pilgrimage to McLean, namely, how difficult it could be to help them.

Medical quality combines knowing what works and delivering it as flawlessly and reliably as possible. A deviation from "routine" (i.e., established standards and protocols of care, including those of patient safety and treatments) can happen with VIPs, compromising the optimal routines of a hospital. Standardization is a core principle of quality, in all fields—from manufacturing to medicine. If proven clinical practices are not held to with great fidelity, if they are changed to accommodate VIPs or others, these patients are at risk for less-than-optimal care.

Moreover, I had seen how many patients who were uprooted to a distant and unfamiliar city far from family and home to a psychiatric setting often experienced the loss of the familiar and the anxiety of the unfamiliar. I did not listen to the voice in my head, and the hubris of my hospital community did nothing to mute it.

On my call with Dr. M, he introduced himself and said he specialized in internal medicine. His English was good, though he was a man of few words. He generally traveled with members of the royal family. He had known Princess W since she was a teenager. He went on as follows (I paraphrase and protect privacy):

> *The princess's problems date back many years. It is hard for me to recall a time she was not a problem, though this is the worst we have seen. As a teenager, she was unruly. Her father thought she would never be able to marry. He (and her mother) sent her abroad to study. When she seemed to have "settled down," her marriage was then arranged to a businessman.*

The marriage did not last long. When it ended, she became depressed, and frequently insolent with her parents. Her brothers and sisters tried to support her, but without success. She began to seclude herself in her palace apartment, seldom coming to dinners or social events, as was expected. She liked to dress up in Western clothing, wear makeup, and go to resorts or other countries where the cultural norms for women were different, more open. Over time, she became more sullen, angry, and impulsive.

Dr. M went on to say that the princess also was coming late to state functions and had been loud and hostile to guests. He said she also seemed to be "staggering about." He and her family thought she might be using drugs, in addition to her being depressed. Her public displays were a "great embarrassment" to the family. "She must have had her servants get the drugs," he continued. The servants had been "threatened" by palace guards to not get her drugs, "street drugs" hence unknowable. She must have intimidated and bribed them.

Some months prior, he went on, the family had Dr. M arrange for a psychiatrist to consult on her case. Dr. M added the following:

First, she refused to see him. But then she obliged, perhaps at the urging of her mother or maybe because she was so unhappy, I don't know. When they met, she hardly said a word. The psychiatrist diagnosed her as depressed and had concerns about her taking her life. He prescribed medications. I will get you details on what he gave her; though, at first, we doubted that she took any. We then had her medication supervised

*to ensure she took what was prescribed. But without
benefit: In the past few weeks she has hardly left her
bed. She has lost weight.*

*The family and I are concerned [he continued]
that she may erupt again—appear inappropriately at
a public dinner or do something terrible to herself. We
understand that your hospital can determine what is
wrong and treat her for her problems.*

I thought, what might they expect? Again, it was a warning
shot to myself, unheeded.

For many patients, the active involvement of their families (see
chapter 4) is essential, an aspect of care that seemed beyond possibility with the princess's family. Moreover, how could we turn what had
become her experience at home (and with transport to a US hospital) into a treatment partnership with her, one she could trust? Even
if we could do all of that, with good clinical results, there would be
the challenge of sustaining her gains upon her return home.

I asked Dr. M what he thought about my arranging, instead,
for a McLean or Boston psychiatrist to go see her in her native
country and environment. He politely but firmly opposed this
idea. He said, "How could her family explain a Western psychiatrist showing up?" There would be no way to prevent even more
gossip. No, he declared, she would need to come to the States. He
thought they could persuade her.

I wonder, sometimes, about the magical expectations people
have of psychiatrists or famous doctors or hospitals. Do we foster
these? Princess W, I had to infer, was a person with serious emotional
problems dating back to her adolescence, now likely complicated by
illicit drug use. She would have to be pressured into coming, which
would not auger well for the "treatment alliance," fundamental to

therapy, as well as the daunting work of recovering a life that long ago had gone awry. Yet, I also wondered how a place like McLean, with its expert medical and nursing staff, could do.

I needed to formulate a plan with realistic expectations and the possibility of success. I suggested to Dr. M that we arrange for Princess W to be admitted to McLean for a few weeks, during which time we would evaluate her psychiatric, substance use, and medical problems. This stay would enable us to offer not only diagnostic impressions, but treatment recommendations as well. We might begin treatment during her stay, like starting her on medication, as well as suggest other therapeutic (cognitive and wellness) approaches that could continue upon returning home. Dr. M asked who would be in charge of her care. I said, "I would be," surprised with myself since I had not decided that before the call. It was infrequent I assumed the care of a particular patient, in good part because of my day-to-day clinical and administrative responsibilities. But I was intrigued. Likely, I suffered from the hubris that made me think I could make a difference. Dr. M responded:

> *I am very pleased that you personally will be the princess's doctor. I will speak with her family and with her. In the meantime, can you look into arrangements for her stay? She requires private quarters and would come with two or three servants. I would accompany her and stay a few days. I would need arrangements made for my quarters in a nearby hotel. I will call you again in a day or two.*

Two or three servants? Private quarters? Now I was on totally new ground. There are small cottages on McLean's 246 acres, but these were for patients whom we knew well and did not need close supervision. In the real world, the princess needed to be a hospital inpatient, with its safety and medical routines, as well as the twenty-four-hour nursing and aide staffing that this entailed. If we deviated from standard procedures, especially those developed to maintain safety, and she made a suicide attempt or obtained and used drugs, we would have failed our own standards—not to mention having an incident on our hands that would cross the ocean to her country. By some good fortune, it turned out that there was a small section of an existing inpatient ward in one of the modernized buildings that was not currently in use; we could adapt that for the princess and her cortege. It would be private yet aligned with the daily workings of the hospital and its nursing staff. Expensive, yes, but that was what they wanted, and I considered that wise. Price did not matter.

FIRST IMPRESSIONS

At the gate at Logan Airport, Princess W was dressed in a designer pantsuit with high heels. She had no warm coat, since, I guessed, she didn't plan to be outside. She exuded the fragrance of perfume. Her hair was pulled up into a careful bun. She wore makeup that helped hide her pallor and thinness. Despite her efforts at looking well, even glamourous, her eyes were glassy, her facial muscles tense, and her demeanor downcast. She limply shook my hand and said not a word.

Then I saw how the princess barked at and tyrannized her servants, how little sway the doctor (who had come with her) had with her. I was stunned by the huge amount of luggage the airport porters soon appeared with, including a huge crate. After loading the cargo that could fit in the van (and car), our caravan drove through the winter flurries that had begun to add glitter to a crisp Boston afternoon.

It was a long forty-five-minute ride to the hospital.

ARRIVAL

I had arranged for several staff to meet us when we arrived at the hospital. A senior nurse greeted us. She would work the day shifts, assist with nursing assignments (and safety protocols), arrange blood and other laboratory services, attend to dietary considerations, and the like. McLean's Internal Medicine Department would provide the initial medical evaluation. Princess W, our flood of attention notwithstanding, was haughty and wanted nothing to do with the McLean staff. I could proudly see how the nurses were not taking her bait. They would allow her time and privacy to settle in. I planned to be back that evening to speak with her.

To my surprise, the princess was promptly available when I returned. We sat down for tea in the open area in the now closed-off and secure section of the inpatient unit outfitted for her. I wanted to begin taking a history, the first step, when possible, in a good psychiatric evaluation. We began. Her English was good but rusty, so we could communicate pretty well. The family medical and psychiatric history I was able to obtain didn't add much to the diagnostic assessment, since she identified no mental illnesses (and certainly no addictions). I wondered if she did not want to tell me—or, perhaps, was instructed not to since many disorders, psychiatric and medical, have a genetic component to the illness.

When I asked for details about any problems she was having, her conversation evaporated like rain in a desert. After trying a bit, I said it had been a long day and I would return tomorrow. I said, in fact, I would visit daily. And that I wanted to have some colleagues meet with her as well, doctors who were experts in depression and problems with dependence on drugs and alcohol. She glared at me but nodded acceptance. I wondered what leverage the family and the doctor had exercised to get her on the plane to come to McLean, to so alien a corner of her world.

As I walked back to my office, I tried to reassure myself that I had had plenty of difficult first encounters with patients. I recalled one when, as a medical student on an elective in Britain, a hospital inpatient upon my incessant questioning threw a typewriter at me (she missed). My training reminded me, meet patients where they are (emotionally) or a flying typewriter could come my way.

It was Dr. M who briefed me on her medical and psychiatric history. She had been given medications that I thought were poor choices for a depressive illness. She had been put on fulsome doses of a strong antipsychotic medication, which as far as I could tell was being used as a nonspecific tranquilizer since there was no evidence of psychotic symptoms, like loss of reality testing, hallucinations, or delusions. She also had been prescribed a highly sedating antidepressant. No wonder she appeared so lifeless. At least I might help by stopping the antipsychotic medication she did not need (that was draining her of energy and motivation), and, as we talked and I learned more, I considered changing her to a less-sedating antidepressant, if that was warranted. Just those interventions might restore some of the life in her, suppressed as it was by medications.

When I met with Princess W the next day, I told her I thought the medications she had been taking were causing problems, especially sleepiness and slow thinking, and that I wanted to begin changing them. We would add others but only when she and I understood better what the matter was—and only when she agreed to what I might suggest. I saw something change in her eyes. I was not telling her how she would be treated. I was asking her to join me in a search for solutions. As both a woman and a patient, the princess, her royal station notwithstanding, had not been allowed to make decisions for herself. My first opening with her came, no surprise, by engaging her with respect, as an equal partner in her care, not as the passive recipient of various demands.

A few days later, Dr. M left to return to his country and his duties. The princess agreed to stay for a few more weeks. I had to assure her that she would be able to return home; I arranged for her airplane tickets in a symbolic effort to show we meant what we said. Trust must always be won with patients (and of course with the many others who constitute our lives). Certain acts can be catalytic in kindling the fragile human experience we call trust. I imagined that there were experiences in her life, dating back a long time, that left her convinced no one would put her interests first. Her forcefulness and independence as a teenager may have helped make the West appealing, giving McLean a chance. Her time living abroad may well have given her a true taste of freedom, a sense of who she was. She had suffered from depression for too many years. Her substance use seemed to begin after the depression started. Substance use and misuse, alcohol and all manner of drugs, can offer, if transiently, relief of psychic pain. That may be the best a person can achieve as a "solution," but not a lasting one. Depression, unrecognized and untreated, the deeper grow its roots, making for a longer and more demanding road to recovery, if that can be achieved at all. Early identification in primary care and pediatrics, to screen, identify, and treat depression, underway in many practices in the US, is essential to reducing its rate, morbidity, and mortality.

The princess, I inferred, had been using sedatives and stimulants. One psychiatric formulation, useful too, proposes that drugs like these are used as a form of self-medication by people suffering with mental illnesses. Psychoactive substances, of various classes, can be powerful and immediate in diminishing both psychic and physical pain: They work. Thus they are used as ubiquitously as the news reports say.

Ironically, in many Eastern countries, psychoactive substances like opioids, stimulants, sedatives, and cannabis are more available than alcohol. As it was with the princess who paid her servants to buy the drugs: She threatened to beat or dismiss them when they hesitated. From time to time, she had them sell some of her possessions on the black market to finance her habit.

Her depression did not abate. Her use of illicit substances continued, with abortive efforts to quit. More than that was needed for her to recover from her co-occurring mental and substance disorders. She needed treatment *and* to find purpose in her life. Addiction is a powerful siren that pulls people into its grasp and "pirates the brain" (Dr. Nora Volkow). Addiction alters the person whose brain and psychology have become substance dependent: A substance use disorder renders other pleasures—and responsibilities—inconsequential (like family, relationships, and work). A person with addiction becomes singularly focused on obtaining psychoactive drugs at any price to themselves and others. There is an adage, known in the AA community, that when a man takes a drink, the drink takes a drink, and the drink takes the man.

There is no running away from depression, by travel or holiday, since the mood disorder will be a fellow companion. And with addiction, its urgent call to use—the craving—to get high, or to forestall withdrawal become center stage.

The princess's troubles had intensified as her mood and substance disorder took on more gravity. Both she and Dr. M told me that guards had been posted by her quarters to limit her going into more public settings, as well as to try to limit any access to drugs. A golden prison is, nevertheless, a prison.

I spent many hours with her in order for the details of her story to emerge. Psychotherapy is a process of listening and talking, and then listening and talking some more. It takes time for patients to feel safe enough to speak, especially about what is painful and shameful.

The weeks passed quickly. She said she wanted to try a different antidepressant from what she had been prescribed before she came to McLean. I suggested a particular selective serotonin-reuptake inhibitor (SSRI), which likely would not sedate her; she agreed to try it. The princess remarked, as her time in the hospital ended, that she felt less anxious, perhaps from the new medication. I imagined as well from the supportive milieu we had created for her. She gained some needed weight. I thought I saw some light begin to shine in her eyes; I hoped it was not a reflection from the hospital's omnipresent, overhead fluorescents.

LEAVING

She was improving and indeed coming back to life. But what would happen when she returned home? How might she have a good shot at surviving reentry? Of having a different (for her, a better and needed) life? I called Dr. M and reported her progress and shared my concerns. I said that Princess W and I had talked about a plan that might help. I said to him that she needed a goal if she was to stay drug-free and rebuild from years of depression. She also needed, I urged, a continuous supportive presence, at least at first, to serve as the "ego" (that part of the psyche that hews to ration and choice), which for her had for some time proved wanting.

My recommendation to him, and thus to her family, was that she would benefit from having someone serve as a responsible "overseer" of her everyday life and behaviors, someone who could enable her to better muster her own (internal) resources and controls. This would have to be someone other than family or security personnel to help her contain her impulses and addictive behaviors, who would help her find less destructive and more rewarding means of meeting her needs.

So, I suggested that the princess return home with a nurse who would live with her for a few months in adjoining but separate quarters. Should that go well, we would plan for the princess to return to see me again, in Boston. I had a person in mind for this job when I offered up the idea. That was a young (female) nurse, let's call her "Betsy," a remarkable person whom I had worked with at the hospital. I thought she would be up to the challenge and the adventure. She was interested and needed the money to help fund her further graduate education. The notion of my paying a home visit during this interval, by the way, was summarily dismissed: That could not be kept secret, I was told again. My presence there, an American psychiatrist, would further the family's shame.

I asked Dr. M if we could appeal to the princess's family. Would they allow her to spend more time outside of her country? A few days later, Dr. M called to say that her family had approved the plan for a nurse but was very skeptical about her leaving home. They believed she would do worse outside the boundaries set for her. One step at a time was possible, I was told. Wise counsel.

Betsy began spending time with the princess on most days. She would brush her hair, and take tea, go for walks, talk a little, and watch movies with her. Betsy's visa was arranged by the family and another first-class ticket was purchased for her to join the returning party. We also set a date for Princess W and Betsy to return to Boston some months later. Instead, however, of returning to the hospital, the princess would stay at a hotel nearby. During the intervening months, I proposed, the princess and I would speak on the phone twice a week; I would also regularly speak with Betsy to supervise and support her work. Before they left, I, with Betsy present, met with the princess's two servants, one of whom spoke a little English. I sought to enlist them in the effort to keep Princess W away from illicit drugs. I put on my most doctorly manner. I said that if they bought (or delivered) her drugs, that would be like killing her. They listened dutifully and nodded. I have no idea if they even understood what I was saying. Later I thought that if they did, then they surely thought me naïve.

HOME

The princess left McLean for home and family. The months passed, but not exactly as hoped for. Our phone calls became less frequent, then were seldom: The princess would "not be available." Betsy reported good weeks and bad, more so the latter over time. She was convinced that the princess had resumed using drugs. Fights with her family had become more frequent and evident. Then came days when Betsy was not allowed to see her. But there were no major incidents, at least that we heard about. On one of our phone calls, Dr. M told me that though she was "better," they had hoped for more. As had I. I began to sense that we might have won some battles—but were losing the war.

VISIT TO THE DOCTOR (ME)

It was a breezy Boston spring day, with flowering rhododendrons marking the way to Logan Airport, when I again went to meet the princess, Dr. M, Betsy, the entourage of two servants, and too many bags.

At tea, in the downtown hotel restaurant after we arrived, the princess looked better but not well. Betsy looked as if she had spent a semester abroad, full of excitement and rich with experience, even if rather defeated in her therapeutic efforts. I met with Princess W every evening in her suite or in the restaurant for tea; sometimes Betsy would join us. Only once did we all have dinner together.

It was much like starting all over again because trust needed to be reestablished. The princess knew I knew about the drug use and the family fights. She wanted to avoid any discussion of what for her were her failed efforts. I would often say that addiction was a disease, with predictable and regular relapses, that recovery was indeed possible, but it would be over an extended period of time. I also talked with her about the illness of depression—to try to give her some perspective on how she had shown some improvement, even if there was still more to accomplish. We talked about the summer ahead. I asked if she'd be able to make plans to spend time abroad. With all illnesses, mental, addictive, and medical, it is a doctor's job to keep hope alive. She was often quiet, too quiet. Her eyes had lost some of the luster I thought I had seen some months earlier.

I met with Dr. M privately. I told him I was convinced that if she returned home, without Betsy, that would not auger well. There would be little chance of her not using illicit street drugs and she would continue to find ways to make everyone miserable, including herself. I asked him if he thought it possible that the family might support her living in the Boston area, at least for the months ahead. He didn't bother to say he would check; he curtly told me that would not be possible. They were pulling up their anchors and about to sail away. I was losing Dr. M's alliance and I was about to lose my patient. Family, culture, depression, and addiction conspired to be a collection of forces for which McLean Hospital and this psychiatrist were no match. The family had expected far more than what we had achieved. When I reminded myself about "the massive summit she needed to climb," that proved no consolation.

Before Princess W left some two weeks later, we spoke frankly. Maybe it's better to say I spoke frankly to her and she listened. I tried to reach that part of her that wanted to live, that needed to once again find dignity and believe in a better future. But I saw that she was too emotionally bruised and depleted. Her ability to stand up and fight another round was nowhere to be seen. She turned to me with what poise and conviction she could assume and said she would try. She said we would talk on the phone, that she would return to Boston in two or three months to resume our meetings and see her friend Betsy.

THE AFTERMATH OF HUBRIS

I never spoke with her again. When I called, she was never "available." I called Dr. M, but he was vague and enigmatic. She would not be returning for further treatment at McLean, he told me. He diplomatically thanked me—and "my wonderful hospital staff"—for our help.

A year or so later I heard from another MGH colleague, who had provided medical consultation to her family. He had learned that the princess remained in the palace. He added that her apartment area had sentries always stationed about it—to keep her from getting out and to keep others from getting in. A gilded cage. This was news that pained me, though it was no surprise. I had grown to admire this woman who tried to fight for a life within her complex crucible of privilege, culture, family, and the darknesses of depression and addiction.

By the psychiatric standards I knew and espoused, Princess W received fine care at McLean. A diagnostic assessment was done thoughtfully and with world-class consultations. Her treatment proceeded along the best biopsychological knowledge our science had to offer. We recognized and focused treatments on both her co-occurring mental and substance use disorders. We established an alliance and partnership with the patient, which, I think, served as a beacon for her and for us. She had excellent medical care to complement her psychiatric services. We sustained professional collaboration with the one person we were permitted to contact in her life, the family physician; through him, we also tried (though in vain) to engage her family. We introduced aftercare support by creating supervised home nursing care. We arranged for her follow-up return.

Some might call this a comprehensive treatment plan. But it didn't work. Or we ran out of time before it could. Whatever degree of expert clinical care provided to this VIP was outstripped by the forces of mental and addictive disease and a culture so different from ours.

To this day, I believe the princess's mood and addictive disorders can be effectively treated. I have seen that happen again and again. However, the daunting truth about all medical care, including psychiatric, is that effective treatment insists that the social circumstances permit recovery to be achieved.

Today, we call these the social determinants of health. These generally depict conditions such as poverty, hunger, housing instability, lack of education and opportunity, violence, and the air and water that render us ill. But the social determinants don't stop there. Prosperity and privilege are not assurances against a person's life circumstances ruining the day. Sure, it helps to have resources, no doubt about it. But they alone are not enough.

McLean delivered. We did our jobs. But we could not change the world. That takes more than a mental hospital. And, as a result, what we provided just was not good enough.

As I write this story, and recall the time in which it happened, I imagine that some readers will think of the hubris we (I) evidenced by taking on what was truly a moon shot, and what an indulgence was extended to this woman and her family. And those who think either or both would be right. The really rich, as they say, are different. They get care that others cannot receive. Sometimes, it is even done right.

But what if the privileged care we render could have a halo effect? Is that also hubris? Imagine if we had succeeded. Or imagine when we will. Her success could be evidence for the value of mental healthcare and might extend to others. First, likely others of privilege, but then, over time, more broadly throughout her and other culturally different societies.

That's what a public health approach to illnesses aims to do: to bring standardized, accessible, and effective care (and prevention) to populations of people, not only individuals.

Breakthroughs often start at the top of the social pyramid, one person at a time, until knowledge and momentum create health opportunities for many. Looking back now, I see some of the roots of my becoming a public health doctor taking hold at McLean.

It is a great privilege to be a doctor. Physicians (and, of course, nurses, PAs, social workers, psychologists, and many other health professionals) are given access to those in pain, the almost universal expression (physically and mentally) of illnesses. To their families as well. We are tasked to do all we can to reduce suffering, to improve functioning, and to always be caring to our patients. And to foster hope, whatever the odds.

This ending to the princess's story (so far as I can know) has me and my hospital failing. Yet, I would try again—and have—with other patients, rich and poor, far and near, when the opportunity arose. I hope that is not hubris speaking.

6

BAD APPLES

Personnel problems are the bane of just about every manager or executive. They exact a disproportionate amount of time and tumult, considering how much else there is to do.

Personnel problems include good, decent people who simply don't have the mental or practical tools they need to get the work done. Many, me included, find these the most grinding of personnel troubles because good people are hard to find, and bringing down reality's hammer on them can feel unfair. You know when a colleague is having this type of problem when they start by saying, "They are a very nice person but . . ."

Also quite problematic are people whose aims seldom, if ever, extend beyond what they want for themselves. There is no "fair" deal with them because, for them, it's all about "me, me, me." They have lost sight of the common good. These bad apples can sour the bunch.

Taking needed action, like termination, to rectify a self-centered style of working can carry the risk of revenge, in the form of legally packaged claims and grievances, which bleed management of time and money. Each claim must be taken seriously, however absurd the "charge" against you may be.

Ideologues have been with us for generations, but there may be a new breed around. These are well-meaning, sincere people who have lost the plot, probably never truly saw it, for example, those in a very large collection of our population—who are at both sides of the political divide that is eating away at our country. In successfully running a hospital or school or manufacturing microchips or mayonnaise, there is an essential mission to be followed. It is, however, not political. Stay your course, do your work, and the bad apples will mostly and slowly disappear. Less noise allows for more attention to getting the actual work done.

Differences and difficulty among coworkers, whatever their reasons may be, are part of your job. Even if keeping the work floor going was not in your job description (at least literally), as a leader, it's yours to overcome.

Business and management gurus teach us the convention that problems usually are the result of a flawed system, not the person who errs. In medicine, errors (like the wrong medicine or the wrong person receiving a medication) are examples. When errors derive from how you routinely operate your organization, future risk can be mitigated with a systems approach to diagnosis and treatment.

As a rule, singling out one person or small group for blame (and shame) runs contrary to what we know about "system problems." Malfunction may *appear* to be the result of an individual when it is not. Medication and other treatment errors and AWOLs from a secure site happen when people are caught in the crosshairs of a malfunctioning system. Singling out a culprit does harm in two ways: Someone unduly suffers shame, and the actual source of error isn't fixed.

These, and other personnel and management messes, abound. As you can see about you every day. But what you are apt to miss because they are blessedly infrequent are the bad apples. These are bad and exploitative characters, often practiced in their game. When someone rotten comes along, they can do great damage to your staff and organization.

Such was the story of a bad apple doctor at McLean capable of bringing disgrace to the hospital, which already had enough trouble from its financial crisis. A bad apple event can be the proverbial straw that can break your back.

DR. SURPRISE

"Dr. Surprise" (name changed, of course) was relatively new to the McLean medical staff. I had met him in the course of hospital business but had not hired him, since that generally falls to the clinical director of the specialty division where the doctor is assigned.

It was a winter evening, as I recall, when I received one of those "crisis du jour" calls. A patient was missing from one of the inpatient units. "Missing?" I asked the resident on duty who had called. "Yes, since late afternoon," she reported. The patient had been in the hospital for about two weeks, having been admitted for a recurrence of mania, the excited, psychotic state of bipolar disorder (once called manic-depressive illness). The medications prescribed to her, the structured, low-stimulation environment of the ward, and supportive nursing care were working. Her acute illness had begun to quiet, the resident added. Her speech was less pressured, she was not so irritable and sarcastic, and her sleep was normalizing (a sign of recovery from the acute phase of this illness and important in recovering from a manic episode). Her inpatient doctor, I was told, was Dr. Surprise. But efforts to reach him on pager and at home had proven fruitless.

The patient, let's call her "Ms. Missing," had been ill with bipolar illness. With good treatment and family support, she achieved an executive career in a nearby state. Too few people know how many people, in demanding careers, have this illness *and* make lives of contribution.

Her family had arranged for her to come to McLean. We had a reputation (though in need of some polishing) in the northeast from treating many VIPs, Boston-area professors, students, writers, artists, professionals, executives, and celebrities too. I did not ask the resident about the circumstances of her relapse into illness, clearly important but not at the moment of her having gone missing.

I called the unit's psychiatrist in chief (PIC) overseeing her care (Dr. Surprise's supervisor). He had notified McLean security. A search of the grounds had not found her. There were plenty of places to hide on a 246-acre campus with forty-six buildings and large tracts of woodland, though it was winter, and the trees and shrubs were mostly bare. I asked Dr. Surprise's supervisor (let's call him "Dr. Chief") to contact the patient's next of kin, who had referred Ms. Missing for admission. I learned he (let's call him "Mr. Significant Other") was a prominent executive, with a legal background. It sure looked as though we had erred, that something significant was terribly amiss in our care of this patient, so we faced concerns about the well-being of our patient and potential legal repercussions. We had not yet notified the police. Not long after being notified, Mr. Significant Other was on his way to Boston. He wanted to meet the next morning, in my office, with whomever I considered needed to be there. Okay, I said to his intermediary.

What would a good detective do? Start by asking questions of the unit's staff, especially the nurses and aides who were almost always the most informed about whatever might be going on in the lives, moods, and minds of their unit's patients. So, that was how our inquiry began. We assembled a small team to find out what we could and reestablish safety for Ms. Missing. Different members of our team, in steady contact with one another, met with the on-duty evening shift, then with the night shift, and then at the 8:00 a.m. nursing report. Several staff said they noticed Ms. Missing and Dr. Surprise spending an "inordinate amount of time" together. It seemed, they said, that they were "too close" in their encounters with each other. A couple of times, reportedly, this pair was seen in her room, unchaperoned, requiring the nursing staff to intervene.

The whole unit, twenty-four patients, knew by the morning that Ms. Missing had gone missing. Another patient had told the unit nursing director that she had seen the doctor taking this patient off the unit, late the previous afternoon. This was critical information and a body blow to the ethics and ostensible caliber of McLean's clinical care.

There are too many instances where people, women principally but not exclusively, are exploited in relationships marked by a power imbalance. There have been accusations against Harvey Weinstein, Bill Cosby, Roger Ailes—the list is very long in the entertainment and media communities. This type of exploitation also extends perniciously to medicine and to colleges and universities (professors and sports coaches), as well as to faith-based institutions. Exploitation does not stop there since workers of all stripes can be subject to the malfeasance of their employers.

Members of my profession, psychiatrists and other mental health professionals, add to the list of those who have used and abused patients. The few who violate this no-nonsense medical ethic taint many other dedicated physicians and institutions. But it happens. And it was happening in my hospital. A bullet of whatever size to the chest can be terminal.

Our meeting with Mr. Significant Other went on as scheduled later that morning. I kept the attendees to clinical staff, no need for lawyers—at least not at that moment. Our hospital staff would focus on finding our patient, using all the resources we could muster. We needed to protect our patient from further harm. This was the first McLean doctor-patient elopement, as far as we knew. The patient's significant other was appropriately outraged. I sensed, nevertheless, that he knew we were determined to make things right, even if after the fact.

We informed the local Belmont, Cambridge, and Boston police about the pair having gone missing. They would scout for Dr. Surprise's car, which likely would tell us where they had eloped to. Mind you, this was before cameras were installed on city blocks, capable of reading and reporting license plate numbers. Absent cameras, the police began a painstaking search process, which takes time, but often works. After a day of searching, the Boston police found his car on a quiet, downtown side street. The precinct shift commander deployed detectives and patrol cars to stake out the area. Soon the police had visual evidence of the doctor and patient leaving and returning to what was a rental building. We had found them. They were going about their new courtship, clandestinely.

It was time for a plan. We would stage an intervention, late that evening, when patient and doctor likely would be at the apartment, and with little going on in this residential area. The police needed to gain entry into their apartment. That was their role, but not more, since upon entry the moment becomes medical care, not law enforcement. We also needed a doctor (other than me, his senior boss, who would fire him) to be there to complete what was called a "pink paper" (referring to the color of a Massachusetts involuntary, psychiatric admission form). That would permit an ambulance to transport Ms. Missing back to McLean, hopefully with little fuss. Two experienced hospital aides joined our intervention team; nonprofessional (lay) aides are less of a threat and more likely to be accepted by a patient than professional staff. They would be able to talk with and engage our patient, more so than the police, even doctors. We asked our McLean staff to *try* to explain to her that she had been victimized by this doctor and that was now over. It seemed like a good plan, though not rehearsed, or informed by prior experience. But we had found the right McLean staff to do the job.

There was, however, the matter of Dr. Surprise. What about him? Did we leave him standing there, agape? Or what? As far as we knew, he had no history of violating medical ethics, of tossing his career overboard, and no known complaints against him (we knew this from the credentialling process he had undergone to obtain membership to the McLean medical staff).

I professionally knew the psychiatrist who led the Massachusetts Impaired Physicians Program. Its focus principally is for doctors who had developed an addiction and who could be helped, voluntarily, to enter treatment. If that took, the doctor would be very carefully monitored, even more so if they sought to return to practice. Addiction is a disease, not a failure of will or character. Doctors are at risk, maybe more so than others, to addiction and its consequences. As far as I and other colleagues at McLean knew, Dr. Surprise was not using substances. But he was acting in an impaired manner, so I called my colleague heading this program. He offered to join the intervention team; now, that is a doctor dedicated to giving others a chance.

I called the medical director, my counterpart, at a nearby private psychiatric hospital. I laid out the story and asked if that information had him consider Dr. Surprise impaired. He did but could only make that determination by exam. If he agreed to hospitalization and arrived in a separate ambulance with EMTs (but no McLean staff), would he be admitted? I was told, yes, for evaluation, which seemed fair given how little we knew about what had prompted this doctor to run off with his patient. Did he have a mental illness or substance disorder? That's a diagnostic question that could be answered in a short time in a psychiatric hospital. We arranged for a second ambulance to arrive for him.

Then, as in a well-choreographed event, all the players assembled on that quiet Boston side street. I was not there for the intervention. Mine was the groundwork and follow-up, not the on-the-ground work. And there was more for me to do to try to ensure an uneventful return at the hospital.

That mélange of professionals did their part. Thankfully well. Ms. Missing, I was told, readily agreed to return to McLean. I imagined by then she had realized that she could do better than being holed up with a boundaryless psychiatrist in an unknown neighborhood without any future plans. Dr. Surprise was indeed agape, I was told, when he opened the door to find the police. Yet, when the doctor from the Impaired Physicians Program gave him the opportunity to go to a psychiatric hospital for evaluation, he agreed, no pink paper necessary.

We re-admitted Ms. Missing to a different McLean inpatient unit, though her adventure was hard to keep a secret. I wondered if other patients likened her to Randle McMurphy, the character that Jack Nicholson played in *One Flew Over the Cuckoo's Nest*, or perhaps to the asylum patients in the French film *King of Hearts*, starring Alan Bates. Though, of course, there was no retribution for our missing patient to face. Instead, she was assigned a new psychiatrist and her treatment resumed, which was with a mood stabilizer known for its effectiveness with bipolar disorder—but not ECT (electroconvulsive therapy), as was the fate of McMurphy in *Cuckoo's Nest*.

Mr. Significant Other stayed in town a couple more days, until satisfied that McLean had regained its footing with our patient. I met with him again before he left. I can't say his outrage had abated, nor that it was "all's well that ends well." But we had solved the immediate problem, like professionals, a standard I believed he considered we had met because he accepted McLean resuming treatment, and Ms. Missing agreed. He told me he would help her find outpatient aftercare, to begin when we deemed her able to leave the hospital. Even though her treatment was back on track, imagine how her trust in doctors would be shaken. Her impaired judgment and shame about her behavior would be matters ahead for her to face and understand to prevent another time when she was at risk of exploitation. But Ms. Missing was doing well, clinically, her acute illness was resolving. It would be better for her to leave McLean as soon as that was safe, a view consonant with a strength-based approach to treatment and recovery and not inviting the regression that can and does occur when hospital stays are longer than needed (also consonant with the McLean we were rebuilding). Shame too can abate when someone starts doing what they can take personal pride in. She was discharged, improved. We never heard from Ms. Missing or her family again.

QUALITY REVIEW

It is customary, in hospitals driven by quality imperatives, to review serious incidents like this one (and many others), always looking to find ways to reduce future risks. I chaired our Quality Review Committee. We met and went through all the details of this incident, as a team of doctors, nurses, and other professionals. Still, without a lawyer in the room because we were focused on understanding and improving our practices, not on averting a lawsuit. Curiously and consistently, the greatest protection against a medical malpractice suit was acknowledging an error and seriously doing what could prevent its future occurrence.

We left the Quality Review meeting with plans (throughout the hospital) for tighter "checks," the regular direct observation of inpatients (from continuously, to every fifteen minutes, to thirty minutes, or one hour) that aides and nurses routinely did and recorded for safety. That included a head count to assure that no one was missing, hiding, or engaged in harmful behavior. This additional structure and surveillance would help avert a number of adverse events. Though with events as rare as a patient missing with her doctor, it is hard to quantify the degree to which safety would be improved by diligent "checks." But when statistical significance cannot be achieved because there are not sufficient data, we ought not to forget about common sense.

We also determined to set about fostering a culture of communication among unit staff. Not quite "If you see something, say something," but close to that. There were boundary violations that had happened, witnessed by staff, but not discussed at shift reports. It takes a culture of nonjudgmental, open communication among all staff to allow for speaking up about what one sees, without fear of retribution from the hospital hierarchy or of having said something that proved not to be so. Both aims are crucial to achieving quality in all settings, not just hospitals. We could lay a new foundation for communication throughout the hospital.

Again, because elopement of this sort is so rare, it is not possible to determine statistically if our ideas and actions prevented another such episode. It did not happen again in the remaining years I was at McLean. But our plans were implemented (not hard to measure) and we had taken another critical step in making McLean safe for other patients at risk for harmful behavior by themselves or others. We were implementing the nonjudgmental approach to improving the quality of our care that works. That's no small achievement in the wake of an event of this nature.

The day after Ms. Missing returned to McLean, I terminated Dr. Surprise's McLean Hospital appointment and salary. I also had his office emptied, though I was told there was nothing personal there. Security was notified that he was made PNG (persona non grata, not welcome at McLean) and was to be denied entrance if he returned, which he did not, so far as we could tell. Human Resources would contact him about his rights regarding health insurance and any other benefits he had from the hospital. In other words, his was a complete firing—on the basis of his vastly inappropriate and endangering professional behavior. Our legal office notified the state medical licensing board about Dr. Surprise's conduct; they said they would "look into it." I had hoped for more.

I also heard from my counterpart medical director at the hospital where Dr. Surprise had been admitted. Evidently, he showed no evidence of acute mental illness or substance dependence and was discharged after about a week. Dr. Surprise sought no aftercare, nor was he in touch with the Massachusetts Impaired Physicians Program. "Lost to follow-up" is the customary term for what became of Dr. Surprise.

What especially perturbed me was that no red alert was added to his medical license. In effect, no substantive documentation was created to inform future employers of his problems. That type of communication is better today but continues to be limited by privacy rights and limited organizational capability to enforce any sanctions.

COMPLAINT

Fast-forward to a couple of months later. My office received a call from a senior attorney at the Risk Management Foundation, asking me to call back when available, which I promptly did. A complaint had been lodged against me, said the attorney who would represent me, filed at the Massachusetts state office responsible for claims of discrimination, of all sorts, including age discrimination, my alleged offense. The complainant, Dr. Surprise, maintained that I had terminated him because of his age, though he was far from his fifties, no less sixties or seventies. I couldn't help recalling a *New Yorker* cartoon about the "national pastime" in our country, namely suing people.

While I refrained from giving Dr. Surprise a diagnosis in my head, I concluded that his professional ethics and sense of personal responsibility were in very short supply. Psychological theory teaches us that one way to elude accountability, personal blame if you will, is to turn it outward: to hold someone else responsible for whatever your predicament may be. Once on that externalizing soapbox, it is a small step to then seek revenge, including compensation, for whatever "damages" could be trumped up. But Dr. Surprise would have to prove his complaint, since US law does hold a defendant (me, in this case) "innocent until proven guilty." That said, my counsel and I would have to prepare my rebuttal and appear in court.

My Risk Management attorney spent hours with me preparing my case. I cannot recall if Dr. Surprise had an attorney or was arguing his imaginary case himself. Is a doctor subject to age discrimination? One feature of American justice is that (civil and administrative) suits generally can be pursued within wide margins. Thus, I had to seriously make my case—before an administrative judge of the Commonwealth of Massachusetts. A date was set, some months later.

COURT

It felt surreal. I was standing before the bench of an administrative judge in a downtown Boston courtroom: accused of age discrimination by a doctor, the psychiatrist whom I had fired from McLean Hospital.

I was represented by highly capable attorneys at Harvard's Risk Management Foundation (RMF), the insurance entity created to cover all the Harvard hospitals and their doctors, including McLean. I knew some of their counsel professionally from my role at the RMF as a psychiatrist advisor. That (unpaid) position came my way because I was the medical director of Harvard's only psychiatric hospital, the defendant hospital in *most* of the mental health claims waged against all the Harvard hospitals.

Hence, I had firsthand reason to be confident about my counsel. And in an ironic way, I was glad to have an independent judge assess the facts and the action I took against the doctor I had fired (not a pleasant action to take).

The judge appeared to have read Dr. Surprise's written complaint about me, which she had before her, and took note of it from time to time. I recall her asking for a few pieces of information from him before turning to me. The judge also had a wealth of McLean documentation about this entire episode of impropriety, as well as what we had done to reclaim our role and responsibility with the patient. Of course, there were materials about the action I had taken to fire him. Still, she wanted to hear the story from me. I welcomed that—not because I felt guilty, but rather I wanted to have the opportunity to openly present the facts and have an impartial judge determine if my decision to fire him was correct. That's called validation and casts a wide halo.

I began telling the story. The judge let me go on for a while. But she was not about to let my testimony be prolix, with unnecessary detail. She urged me to move along with the story, and I did. I think I spoke for less than ten minutes. There was no counter from the plaintiff. To my amazement and appreciation, the judge, right there and then, said, "Case dismissed."

My counsel and I filed out of the courtroom. We went to a nearby diner for coffee. Had we "won"? Yes, in the limited sense that my action was vindicated, and I (actually my insurer, the Risk Management Foundation) was not about to pay this doctor for his charge of age discrimination. Yet, what would be the consequences for him? While he was out of his current job, he still had his medical license. He could move, in Massachusetts or to another state, and go back to work, putting other patients in peril. Justice, at best, was far from complete.

As I write this tale, many years later, we still regularly hear reports of doctors exploiting patients. Joe Nocera, a *New York Times* reporter, had a hugely popular podcast called *The Shrink Next Door*. It was about how an NYC psychiatrist thoroughly and shamelessly exploited his patient—taking over his Hamptons house and using his patient as its caretaker.

Other stories like that regularly appear in the press. Some in my profession (ours is not the only one, but the one I think most about) have been exposed for their egregious behaviors. They used the power inherent to the doctor-patient relationship for their own interests, not the patient's. Not only did they fail to live up to the Hippocratic oath of "first, do no harm," but they are also left free to prey again.

Surely, the psychiatric profession with its licensing and regulatory functions needs to do a better job of protecting those who seek our care. Maybe psychiatry needs its own type of "Me Too" movement?

7

NEW MANAGEMENT

There is no standard playbook for change. But there are well-considered and useful books about the milestones of change, how (and with whom) to light the fire and keep it going, and markers for uphill and when the rest is downhill. These are not meant to be a map to follow. Instead, they offer a compass for when radical change produces its disorienting effects. They are good nightstand books that either will upset your sleep or serve as soporifics.

Business books about change and management use a language that goes directly to our prefrontal cortex, where reasoning and judgment, no small matters, are purported to reside. But what about our brain's amygdala, a rather small region deep in the brain and its up close and personal relationship to the hippocampus? It's the amygdala that regulates our emotions and the hippocampus that encodes memory, especially memories of personal experiences that will shape our future.

I am finally getting to the point.

There is no single, comprehensive "theory of change." But there is a report from the front lines by a world-class change agent, which resonated with my experience of the tumultuous years at McLean that I have tried to convey in this chapter. That change agent was Mahatma Gandhi.

Gandhi helped lead a huge nation to freedom and democracy. One comment he made reveals the bruising, ironic, and sweeping experience of how a culture is transformed. It happens in stages, too, and especially when change threatens those in power and stands to topple an existing culture. His comment was "First they ignore you. Then they shame you. Then they fight you. Then you win." More below.

FIRST THEY IGNORE YOU

You likely have witnessed a street scene when an American tourist is lost in a foreign country, where many of its citizens don't speak English. The tourist hails a passerby and asks, for example, "How do I get to the train station?" The native looks at the tourist quizzically and says nothing, to which the tourist responds by raising his voice, amplifying the sound as if the intended receiver were across a wide expanse of river. The tourist never imagines it was not a matter of hearing, but of comprehension.

At first, I guess I (and some of my leadership colleagues) did some raising of our volume with those perplexed by our Paul Revere routine, though about the invasion of corporate healthcare rather than the British. But then we stopped. The title of the 1958 film *Run Silent, Run Deep* captures the approach we then took. We needed to run our planned course silently and with the depth it required. Then the clinical and fiscal reports began to paint catastrophe. Then it was no longer possible to ignore that McLean Hospital was entering a state of what in medicine is called a Code Blue, namely in need of resuscitation. That wasn't long, about a year.

THEN THEY SHAME YOU

Shame is at its most painful when delivered ad hominem. Humiliation is always personal, even when applied to more than one person.

Dr. Mirin was first in line. No matter that he had been an accomplished researcher and clinician at McLean, not so many years earlier. He was now like the Angel of Death at McLean, even when that was a death that we could avoid. Blame the messenger.

Pointed like a spear, there were assertions of: self-interest, a shallow appreciation of McLean and its culture, and sophomoric plans for the future of its clinical services. As a rule, it's not a good idea to try to respond to unproven and debasing claims. Responding would send us deeper into the mire, not unlike answering the question "When was the last time you beat your wife?"

I hardly had a foot in the door when Mirin informally put me, an unknown and an outsider, in charge of clinical services with its many acclaimed doctors (and those who thought themselves to be). What bad judgment, what disrespect for the "elders," claimed those doctors who previously had made for McLean's national, even international, resplendent reputation and success.

Just for the record, I had no ethical or legal complaints against me; I was an open book in the Boston and Cambridge communities, where I had worked in three Harvard teaching hospitals for thirteen years before McLean, already an author of six professional books and, when I began at McLean in 1989, the president of the 1,800-member Massachusetts Psychiatric Society.

Mirin and team were the ne'er-do-well guys who would "destroy" McLean's quality of care, so richly deserved and sustained, as it was—but not anymore. One rhetorical hammer was the question "How could *anyone* benefit from fourteen-day hospital stays?" After all, at McLean, it took *at least* thirty days to do a "proper" patient evaluation (treatment came after that). Long inpatient stays had been McLean Hospital's great distinction, though there was no proof of their effectiveness.

If we were successful in making our changes, the criticism went, McLean would no longer be sought as a haven for poets and movie stars, for Harvard and MIT professors and students, and for Mayflower descendants. Would the celebrities stop coming to a hospital with a population of those diverse in color and socioeconomic station? What would become of the flush clinical revenues (that was dated, but no matter) and the rich, connected donors? We were "destroying" the famous McLean Hospital. We were creating a staff practice, to do what had been the domain of the private practice doctors. We were going to charge rent for on-campus doctors' offices!

My "ignorance of" and "disregard for McLean's legendary, quality care" was a way to spray shame paint all over me, my boss, and our colleagues in the yellow brick building.

Shame was what the British poured onto Gandhi (not that we were "Gandhis"). Shame is easy to apply and hard to defend against. Be ready, because it will come at you when making radical change, which has its "winners" and "losers."

We believed we would prevail by unrelenting and smart problem-solving, every day and in every way. But that is hard to do with a scarlet letter and your fingers crossed as well.

THEN THEY FIGHT YOU

Stories resplendent in war abound in personal tales, books, and films that reveal noble human qualities such as loyalty, courage, determination, and brotherhood.

I still, though infrequently, relive in my dreams what must then have felt like McLean trench warfare, each side dug in, with gains often measured in feet, not even yards. There were battles without names that we had with other professionals, organizations, and institutions. It's small stuff, compared to a whole country seeking freedom from 200 years of British Empire rule. But Gandhi was there, through to the "last mile," fasting once again, when India won its independence in 1947. He was like my North Star.

Our leadership group did not exactly welcome having to battle, but battle we did, "white glove" (maybe "white shirt") battle. We battled about the clinical model of care, program expansion, for a more diverse patient population, and clinical services at McLean. For the patience needed to exit our fiscal nightmare.

Then they fight you. For McLean's executive and senior leadership team, "they" were varied groups of professionals, the "system" of the corporatization of psychiatry, and the powers that governed this Harvard hospital.

We knew the battles would subside and the sun once again would shine on McLean Hospital. That took about five years, not 200, but those five were dog years.

THEN YOU WIN

Every win comes at a cost. There was an exodus of some long-standing McLean attendings who took their clinical and teaching gifts with them. There was the ever-shrinking of inpatient hospital clinical services. There was finding ways to withstand the corporate invaders. We strived to stay alive yet stay true to patients, not put profits first. We wanted to restore the place where, if needed, you would want your loved one to go for psychiatric treatment.

We saved McLean Hospital, which, well over twenty years later, is prospering on all its fronts: clinical, research, and training.

HERE'S THE "A" TEAM THAT DID THE JOB

My new boss, Steven Mirin, MD, in his inimitable manner, had told very few people at McLean he had hired me, no less as the future medical director (if I measured up). Steve had a tough hide, a big heart for those genuinely in need and whom he could trust, and considerable facility with "at the moment" wry humor. The hide would do him well at McLean. He has been one of the two great bosses I would know—and I have had quite a few bosses. By the way, two years after he left McLean, I joined him in Washington, DC, where he had gone to head up the American Psychiatric Association. Imagine, someone putting up with me twice.

I had set up camp at McLean and began to stack my schedule with lots of meetings with our professional staff, mostly with individuals, some in pairs. Forgive the baseball metaphor, but I needed to know the players as I assumed my role as clinical general manager of this famed Harvard hospital. I needed to know who batted left, who right—the switch-hitters too, the pitchers with a fastball and those with a curve, those who had done well at bat and those who too often swung and missed, and, critical to our mission, the team captains and morale boosters. As fitting the metaphor, our executive team faced a seemingly endless season of 162 games, unlike power-housing through the seventeen (regular season) games of an NFL season.

McLean, its roster of first-rate players notwithstanding, had begun losing. It was upon the new hospital administration to give (most of) our professional players a more contemporary game to play—and win. Our campaign to be an acute care hospital would require the predominance of clinical staff to play a different game of "baseball." We also would need to identify those facile enough to successfully "relocate" from their existing service (e.g., geriatrics, mood disorders) to another where they were greatly needed (e.g., admissions, psychosis services), and those ready to advance to greater professional responsibility.

As I met the players, few offered more than a patient ear. Diversity of opinion was the rule, not the exception. The feet and lips of many of our clinical colleagues were waiting to see what would happen, whether they would join, be swept along, or dodge the changes in psychiatric practice underway. What would be the hospital's next chapter, and theirs as well? Why jump, if you didn't know where to, how, and how far? That said, those who delivered and professionally achieved the most were actively involved in creating their new roles. They were the swift and the bold: the ones to harness themselves to a cause.

Once the snowball of change started down the hill, the most common request was not about role or direction. It was about *pace*: "Don't go so fast." We had to convince many that speed in change was essential to our survival, even if we knew a more measured pace would allow for an initial, deeper adoption of changing standards of medical care (and their measurement). There was no rock and a hard place, only the new McLean way, or the highway.

Few at McLean, including a number of the senior doctors and administrators, knew me personally. Why I was at the hospital, and what I was doing, must have baffled them. Though that allowed for surprise, which can undo many a mask. No meet and greet, just play ball.

My day often started with a brief, sometimes a "drive-by," meeting with Mirin, who could be very funny and dead serious at the same time. Levity is an underappreciated dimension of a successful chief.

My next stop was with my new administrative assistant to itemize whom she would call to set up my meetings, conveying urgency, that time was finite. An unremitting sense of urgent need is requisite to being a strong leader; Mirin had that covered (and I was not far behind). The medium *is* the message, *now*, because time is not boundless. As Richard Rohr, who wrote on spirituality, said, "Without a sense of urgency, desire loses its value."

My initial rounds were with the doctors, psychologists, social workers, and nurses who were the senior clinical leaders of the hospital. Many were famed clinicians, researchers, and clinical administrators. I would make friends—and foes. Sometimes, I had trouble judging if a colleague's words meant they were friend or foe. But action, or inaction, would tell.

There is an adage about academic politics that states how bruising the going can be—ironically, often because there is so little at stake. The McLean upheaval, however, was far more consequential. It was not posturing or politics; it was coming to grips with what had to be done, against a backdrop of a house on fire.

Rohr also proffered, "What the ego hates more than anything else is to change—even when the present situation is not working or is horrible. Instead, we do more and more of what does not work."

We know that a chain's strength is as strong as its weakest link. We needed a team where all the players were on the "A" list. Every link needed to be as strong as the others because resistance to change is ubiquitous and apt to focus on the person most likely to bend or break.

An "A" team member thinks independently and acts collectively, is the self-starter who comes to your office with an idea. This team member has a big work ethic too. Building, supporting, and sustaining the senior leadership was no idle matter. Hard decisions about whom to keep and whom to let go are not meant to be benevolent to individuals; that's charity—a virtue that has little sway after an asteroid strikes.

The McLean "A" team was built, trimmed, and rebuilt, especially early on, when we were climbing out of an organization hole beset with confidence and morale problems. Every change had to improve our game. We began to look like a team that could win, no longer in last place but far from first. But moving on (out) members of your team was not easy when you cared about your colleagues, which was usually the case.

"Team" can either be a slogan, a way of eluding individual responsibility. *Or* it can be more than the sum of its parts.

Effective teams often have a chemistry you can feel. They are not born at the top of their game: That comes step-by-step, as their "flywheel" (thank you, Jim Collins) gains momentum.[11] Their imperative is being effective, GSD (Getting S—t Done), which applies in countless settings, including hospitals, the military, corporations, educational institutions, among emergency responders, and so many others. An effective team has a common and clear purpose: to survive, to win, to make money, to save lives, to innovate and create, or to defend against today's common foes

---

11   Jim Collins and Jerry I. Porras, *Built to Last: Successful Habits of Visionary Companies* (New York: Harper, 2002).

(human, microbial, and environmental). That purpose, like a military mission, must have clear, feasible, and measurable objectives. When purpose is clear (and crisp), a few choice words can tell your story. Which allows for taking control of the narrative; don't bore of restating your elevator (or stump) speech, since repetition is a core element in learning. It is a common purpose that ignites the chemistry of bonding and builds trust. There is no shame in trying and stalling out or failing along the way. Having no "misses" means you are not trying hard enough.

That's what we built at McLean. Not the team that first took the field, but the team that added talent and off-loaded those who were not made for an "A" team or for our mission. Soon enough, with a little "spring training," we had our starting lineup, which included the following:

Our boss, Steven Mirin, MD, an unshakable source of drive and support to our executive team in planning and implementing clinical and organizational change. Mirin's troubles were greater than any of the members of his executive team, including mine. He knew the hospital would soon begin to hemorrhage money, something his board of directors would not welcome—though they needed to permit because a lot more time was essential to re-create McLean Hospital. Mirin's ironic humor was invaluable, at least for me, to withstand the resistance and criticism that would come our way. I spent more time with him, for many years, than I did with my family at the time.

There was the unstoppable Philip Levendusky, PhD (now retired). Phil led the Psychology Department at McLean, a stellar program for clinical psychology grad students. He also led the behavioral treatment unit for people with serious obsessive-compulsive symptoms, eating disorders, and intractable depression. Nevertheless, his portfolio soon substantially grew. He is one of the most entrepreneurial people you will meet. Over the years ahead, he developed and implemented over forty new clinical programs on and off the McLean campus.

No one can save a business (including a medical enterprise) in a death spiral if all you do is cut. Here is where leadership is put to a different test, that of spending money to stop losing money. Yet the adage "don't throw good money after bad" stalked us, because if our effort failed, our grave would become deeper and wider. Nevertheless, McLean had to grow.

Phil was the engine for McLean's growth of new services. He became vice president (later senior VP) for business development (and later for communications as well). I was proud to contribute, especially on the McLean campus, what I could to successfully implementing a very broad range of psychiatric and substance use services, consonant with a model of acute psychiatric care, and strongly linked to community-based programs and resources. Phil was a builder and keenly able to spot opportunity, both for new services on the McLean campus and in the community. As but one example, to meet the pressing need (more extant today than ever) for child/adolescent services, he devised and led the transfer—rather than dissolution—of the McLean-based Child Inpatient Service to the Franciscan Children's hospital in Boston.[12] Recently, a PGY 4 (fourth year of training) psychiatric resident, soon to be a Child Fellow, told me she was on rotation there, and loving the experience—over twenty years after Phil planted the McLean flag there. Thank you, Phil, for showing us, again and again, that McLean could survive—by ongoing growth.

---

12   "Inpatient Mental Health," Franciscan Children's, https://franciscanchildrens.org/mental-health/inpatient-mental-health/.

Mirin, Levendusky, and I were not, could not, constitute the entirety of our executive "suite." Our total number was closer to a starting lineup of a baseball team.

A hospital cannot function without nurses; many aptly believe they run hospitals (I agree). Linda Flaherty, RN/PCNS (now retired) was given the title (and the responsibilities) of senior vice president of patient care services. That meant heading the Nursing Department and delivering the caliber of experience that patients and their families are due. Linda was usually quiet among us big talkers, but when she spoke, we listened. Her values (e.g., respect, kindness, and attention to detail) needed to be embodied by all the nurses, aides, and clinical services personnel because they are the true north of patient care. Patient care principally is rendered by nurses, who are the most trusted of medical professionals. Nurses have saved my administrative and clinical ass more times than I can remember.

Michele Gougeon, MS, MSc (now retired) was not just another moon orbiting in Mirin's solar system. She was the GSD person. A new building roof, no money? No problem. Countless regulatory and licensing surveys to be not simply passed but excelled at (after all we were a Harvard hospital)? Bring them on. Oh, bad service from our food vendor? They better watch out. Yes, those are for the chief operating officer (later executive vice president—EVP). Michele was a combination of brains and duct tape. Also, generally quiet. Beware those quiet ones.

The McLean Research Division was not in my portfolio, yet, in parallel, pursued the mission of restoring revenues to McLean's bottom line. The research portfolio was a vital source of revenue for the hospital, especially federal grants with their robust indirect recoveries, which could add an additional 50 percent to a grant's direct care payments ($1 became $1.50).

The finances of a teaching, clinical, and research hospital are like a Rubik's Cube, needing a bit of a "wizard to optimize revenue" from an array of payers, like Medicare, Medicaid, commercial insurers, managed care companies, and (for McLean) some private pay, which was dwindling.

David LaGasse became our CFO a bit after 1989, when the bleak financial future of McLean was written in capital letters on a wall of spreadsheets. A dedicated man, he never lost track of the plot. Dave is still at McLean, now as the senior vice president of fiscal affairs and the CFO.

Those were our major players, plus, please don't forget to count me in!

We had to re-engineer—clinically, financially, scientifically, educationally, and operationally—a hospital in a death spiral, though many myopically still thought it was doing just fine.

THE MCLEAN BOARD OF TRUSTEES

On the hospital's organizational chart, over our executive team, was the McLean Board of Trustees, with a great honor going to the chair (unpaid and often a donor).

Substantive organizational change requires unwavering support from its board of trustees—support for the mission and its implementation plan, for the president/CEO, the provision of wise counsel, patience, and financial giving (personally and by their turning to other benefactors) to name a few tasks. Everyone reports to the board, which may not be evident on a daily basis (unless you are Mirin). The board approves all major decisions and casts a long shadow.

Mirin put in legions of time (another demand of a leader) to develop relationships with board members, to keep them continuously informed, especially with the board chair.

NO SURPRISES

When I arrived in 1989, the sitting chair had the genteel air of a Boston nobleman, George Putnam. He was an elegant man, a Protestant, with a distinctly understated, New England manner. His professions had included banking, investing, consulting, and serving as a federal government official. Doing well, in his service to McLean, he also was doing good. He was emblematic of what has been called the Boston Brahmins, the city's elites. He was faithful to governing our psychiatric hospital, while also serving on the board of Massachusetts General Hospital (MGH).

My guess was that he had moored a thirty-foot, teak sailing boat, constructed decades ago in a Massachusetts boatyard, and, while greatly seaworthy, it was not especially built for comfort. Bless George Putnam. He was kind to our executive group, in an avuncular way. I would see him at board meetings and celebratory events, where he was always gracious and welcoming.

I recall the board meeting that marked Mr. Putnam's stepping down as chair. His successor, John Kaneb, was a Catholic, his wealth self-made in energy and corporate leadership. Mr. Kaneb, upon taking on the role of chair, said of Mr. Putnam that a smart businessman "knows when to get in and when to get out." I greatly admired John Kaneb, a manager, deeply dedicated to psychiatry and mental health. You wanted him on your side.

Every once in a while, in the early evening, he would appear at the open door of my office, having met or on his way to meet with Mirin. It was my privilege to invite him in, as I did, of course. Our conversations were brief and like him, to the point. Mostly he praised my work as he knew we were waging a hard, relentless campaign to save the hospital—under his charge as board chair.

But I was the one who needed to praise Mr. Kaneb. I tried,

but he would have none of that. He had taken on the mantle of chair at the time that McLean began its financial free fall. He signed on to brave the years of losing money, under his watch, as changing oversight organizations (MGH, Partners Healthcare, and for-profit corporations circled like vultures—with McLean as their prey. He was a businessman who understood not giving up, surely built from his personal experience. Mirin would talk with him on many an evening, in person or on the phone, especially when a board meeting approached. There was a clear kinship between the Jewish doctor and the Catholic businessman. They both had earned their stations, amid heavy competition, and were focused on their work to a fault. The mantles they both wore were heavy, which each knew, furthering their mutual respect. They knew how to win yet play by the rules.

MY FELLOW TRAVELERS

It would be terribly remiss of me to not acknowledge my gratitude and admiration to McLean's clinical directors and service chiefs (I hope they knew; if not, I archive here my great fortune for their leadership and friendships. They led the complex specialty programs which was how the hospital became organized, including admissions, mood disorders, geriatrics, child psychiatry, women's mental health, substance disorders, eating disorders, residential services, psychotic illnesses, trauma, and more.

They were our field generals, resolute in tackling problems every day. They earned our gratitude, since we in the leadership team saw them create a diverse range of superb clinical services; we also knew about the bullets they dodged or turned into opportunities. Go to www.McLean.org to see the comprehensive array of McLean's programs and services thanks to their leadership.

LEADERSHIP

Leadership is a human endeavor, not born but made. We are human beings, with our strengths and foibles. With the right people in place, we were ready to further accelerate the hard work of piloting McLean to safety and accomplishment.

This chapter is not (only) a trip down memory lane. I mean to illustrate, recognize, and value effective and sustained leadership. We became an "A" team with two rings: those in the yellow brick building and those at the points of patient care. We were there to be of service (which did not need to be said) to our patients and families, who would honor us with their trust.

8

EFFECTING CHANGE

We see people change their minds (and behaviors) all the time. About what to wear, what to eat, where to go. About relationships fundamental to our lives and well-being. About more perilous matters too, like cigarette smoking and suicide. People can change their minds, not because they are racked by doubt and not from being besieged with rationale and science, but because of *ambivalence*.

Ambivalence is different from doubt: It is holding two contradictory views or feelings at the same time. You are not apt to change your mind unless the idea is already there, however available or buried. No one changes another person's mind. Only the decision-maker can change his or her mind. Though a catalyst for change can help, like a trusted friend, family member, or coworker. This trusted other person allows someone to find in themselves their ambivalence, and consider, even arrive at, a polar point of view.

As with all matters human, the best prescription for change is trust. Requisite but not enough.

For change to *stick*, we also need to know *how* to go about making the change. How do you plan to get from A to B to C? Though that too is not enough.

More than change, *transformation*—the epitome of change—would be necessary to save McLean Hospital. That requires the third leg on the stool of change, namely demonstrating ongoing *proof of success*: reliable, verifiable, and continuous proof. To paraphrase the surgeon who first proved ether to be an effective anesthetic (in the Bulfinch amphitheater at MGH), "[This] is no humbug."

Even transitory change cannot be realized by proclaiming to someone what they must do. Telling people what to think or do (or both) stalls out quickly. To the recipient that can feel like uninvited control, propaganda, or indoctrination, all of which fester rebellion. In an organization, for a person to realize a change and sustain it, they must trust their leadership, know how to get from where they are to where change is sought, and see convincing evidence that they indeed have changed. McLean needed red-to-black change on corporate and organizational balance sheets, reliable evidence of improvement in its clinical care, as well as patient and family experiences of the services they received. At 200 years old and in peril of being closed, McLean would settle for no less.

THE STAGES OF CHANGE

If you embark on the bumpy road of change, you likely will encounter a number of influential descriptions (theories) of change.

But first, here are a few helpful theories and descriptions of change that served as guardrails that guided our efforts, *and why*.[13] In the 1970s, two behavioral researchers, Drs. Prochaska and DiClemente, offered their "stages of change." We can see in their early work ways to measure (and later decrease) "unhealthy behaviors" that were the foundation for understanding the organizational change for which they are best known.

For those weathering radical reconstruction, organizational or personal, their stepwise process of "stages" helps by providing milestones along the way. Their "stages" help to bear the slow process of disruptive change by furnishing markers of moving forward (and backward). Over time, a bounty of interventions became associated with what became their final six stages of change (see the following).

Their stages of change focus our attention on people—or populations—who are unaware (sometimes oblivious to what is obvious to others) that their behavior or attitudes can create serious problems, and how, in a stepwise manner, they change, when they do.

Their first stage assesses readiness to change. Determining whether readiness has been achieved can be highly valuable because it is the sine qua non for *all* the subsequent stages. It is the "go" switch in the process of change. Carefully considering why and how readiness was achieved, or its converse, opens the mind's eye to what, for example, led to tottering finances, low morale, often a degradation in performing the core mission, and, for a hospital, patient safety and treatment. After all, *you can't fix what you don't know*. The readiness phase allows for cognitive reframing, for portraying the present troubles from a different, more sanguine

---

13   Author note: These summaries are mine, taken from primary sources; they, thus, reflect my thinking, bias, and experience.

perspective, where what seemed undoable begins to look doable. A change in perspective can fuel motivation and a wish to change, rather than persist with familiar, if destructive, habits.

Their stages, in the following list, are progressive, essential steps along the way. Each stage can also lend itself to specific interventions that further propel movement to adopt the behaviors needed to survive. These, in turn, progressively build the capacity for further forward movement.

AUTHOR'S NOTE

During the long slog of change at McLean, I found myself regularly applying these stages to individuals, friends, and foes, as well as to the progression of my hospital's more adaptive organizational responses. Adaptive responses might include transparency in information and communications, allying with other organizations facing similar problems (and not just other hospitals), and, most notably, that quality improvement initiatives replace blame. I could see McLean being more elastic and skillful in navigating the corporatization of medicine. We were on the right track, even if a day or a week felt otherwise.

The Prochaska and DiClemente method seems to me a map, useful for staying on course, deciding where to go next, and where and when to stop and refuel. A map comes in handy because change is disorienting. And there are the traps change brings, including roaming off the course, a.k.a. "scope creep" (for example, adding on more to do that is not essential to the mission, and thereby jamming momentum), not making needed midcourse corrections, or freezing in place, from whatever were your plans. But keep in mind that the boundaries of each stage, how and when it begins or ends, are *fluid*, and may blend into one another. This approximates real life, which does not fit into rigid boxes to be checked.

These stages can be considered a recipe, which includes all the ingredients, and the sequence needed to deliver up a cake, casserole, or organizational metamorphosis.

Prochaska and DiClemente's Six Stages of Change

1. Precontemplation

2. Contemplation

3. Preparation (Determination)

4. Action

5. Maintenance

6. Termination

No model of the human mind or behavior can be one-size-fits-all. If these principal themes don't serve you well enough, don't get bogged down in the fine print, which is not how actual, personal, or organizational transformation proceeds.

But don't introduce stage 4 (Action) until there has been adequate recognition, readiness, and preparation. Don't "ready, fire, aim." The bullet will be wasted or might ricochet and hit you in the head.

THE NAYSAYERS AND THE INNOVATORS

The McLean story, like its countless brethren, illuminates who can be trusted and sincerely thanked for their contributions, and those ready to pick your pockets or poke holes in your canoe, so to speak. Success would require a steadfast process of financial recovery, growing clinical services and research, and trustworthy evidence that the Olmsted Park mental hospital was improving the lives of our patients and their families.

McLean's transformation effort would be hammered by doubters and naysayers. Those who clung to the view that change was anathema would not do very well over time, not from retribution, but by their own doing.

There were predators, too, who could benefit from the hospital's demise. And there are always some imbeciles in the mix, adding more complexity than color.

Change, as well, does not come without the wounds of battle, mostly borne by its principal drivers: the leadership group at the tip of the spear. Their future, the next chapter for them, is always uncertain. Recall that Winston Churchill, having led the British out of their "darkest hour" to victory, was voted out of the prime ministry once the war was won and the peace treaties signed.

A second dynamically illuminating model of change describes how innovations diffuse throughout a group or organization.[14]

In a group—small or large, homogenous or diverse—be sure to look first for who can be the *innovators*, those who will lead the charge onto the field of battle. They open the doors of change and are the first ones through. Innovators get the flywheel of change moving; they create momentum. Thank them, give them opportunities to grow and take on more complexity and responsibility. They are the future of your institution.

They also draw the attention of the "early adopters," those who have been bystanders, yet open to the need to overhaul the existing conditions that stall organizational achievement. Early adopters

---

14   Everett M. Rogers, *Diffusion of Innovations*, 5th ed. (New York: Free Press, 2003).

are the engine of change. They rattle the bones of a calcified culture, studded with obdurate people; they soften and make more malleable the hard work of change. It is no small feat to uproot deeply held views and convictions. And, in our case, to do so without killing an iconic hospital's identity or draining its vitality.

Innovators and early adopters represent a small minority of your workforce. There is a vaster body of doers, *the early majority*, needed to significantly move the dial of change. Many of these have yet to recognize the institution's dysfunction and the uncertainty of its future. They still are bystanders who can be mobilized to become actors, with specific goals and roles in the progression of change ahead. Without them (and then *the late majority*) the engine of conversion has too few pistons to get to the finish line.

Those in between the past and the desired future, the early majority, are in a lonely place, often lacking a clear and transparent identity or role, because change is fluid. Remember, few people want to be left out: We are group animals. Those who are brought on board can enliven and embolden a transformation and continue to spread its ethos. None of us truly wants to be alone.

The early majority are *not* "resisters." Considering them as resisters creates unneeded adversity and drives people away from you. It's hard, I know, to think of them as observers, taking it all in, biding their time, when they are essential to reaching substantive transformation.

Malcolm Gladwell, the brilliant social commentator and storyteller, called the moment when, for example, these three groups (innovators, early adopters, and early majority) come together, sufficient in size and prepared for action, "the tipping point." That also is the title of his 2000 best-selling book. McLean too would have its tipping point, when we could see the hospital surfacing from its sea of problems. The tipping point is when disparate people, positions, and groups consolidate and are no longer splintered groups. As an ensemble, they are catalytic for success. Once at Gladwell's tipping point, the pace of change accelerates, engaging the predominance of the other hearts and minds needed to drive deep and lasting change.

There are others, firmly rooted in the way things were. Gladwell called this group the "laggards." They resist and are averse to change, seemingly no matter what that might be. Generously, they might be called the determined "naysayers" or "conservatives." But be forewarned; they can consume huge amounts of time and energy, to no avail. Forget about changing their minds. They are not needed to reach the tipping point. Let the laggards lag. Try not to pay attention to what may be their chant or their hurling denigrating words meant to defeat the tide you are generating. Still, it's not easy to ignore the ill will of some of the laggards, as I personally can attest to. I had to remind myself, many a time, that getting baited is a losing game. That's energy better spent advancing the early service and personnel changes underway.

KEY PLAYERS

As early as you can, you need to identify and attend to your roster of key players, for a number of reasons.

First, they are often the ones on another organization's recruitment list, ripe for poaching. If they are your lead players, it is no stretch to imagine them on the draft list of a competing organization(s). They need to know from leadership how valued they are, how they are needed and trusted to be actively engaged in the changes underway. Being valued and participating often count more than money (up to a point), particularly for doctors and other professional staff. It is a kindness, a needed kindness, to explicitly appreciate their work, to thank them and offer gratitude—known to be good for both the one expressing gratitude and the one receiving it. Delegate to them, let them run the ball over a finish line or two. Leadership should not claim credit or pride when it can be honestly accredited to the innovators and early adopters. Successful leadership means effective action by those who occupy the front lines. Learn to smile sincerely and nod, to take pride in your players.

Second, find and make opportunities for professional growth and advancement as standard procedure to grow your future leaders. Build a respectful work culture by acting respectfully yourself. Promote, every time you can, a flexible approach to hours worked, team care, and a work-life balance. These are not intangibles. These are the gold you need to prospect for and distribute; they count a lot to today's workforce, all the more so as a consequence of the COVID pandemic.

Third, use your evolving leaders as your spokespeople; they are far more likely to be heard by colleagues and employees than the administration, who may be dubiously held, even distrusted. Nurses are the most trusted of medical professionals—by other nurses, patients, and families. They are the ones who can safely make house calls, do outreach in neighborhoods known for violence. The residents in a neighborhood known for violence recognize that nurses are there to help—a mother, father, sister, brother, child—someone living in the neighborhood who is suffering, including gang members. A physician would be in trouble, but not a nurse. Trust the nurses to be your eyes, ears, and spokespersons among the hospital's professional and nonprofessional community. Actively seek their input and ideas and use their coaching (of you) to succeed.

Fourth, because there now is a huge workforce shortage in medicine, especially doctors and nurses, remember to always value your people; you cannot afford attrition (especially with the demands of COVID and its role in the departure of first-line clinicians). You already don't have enough people. Recruitment and replacement are a bear and cost a lot of money. Retention and job satisfaction are needed goals for you to pursue.

Hew to the adage that it is better to give than receive. Smarter too.

The story told in this book is applicable to many organizations and settings, particularly when financial instability has eclipsed stability. With the corporatization of healthcare, with its investor-ownership, the primary objective is profit: There is no success or corporate survival without ongoing profitable performance. Healthcare has become a commodity, but that need not mean that the mission of patient care cannot coexist. A full hand of sound ideas and their fine execution would be needed to gain both the public trust and succeed in the business of healthcare. Welcome to the state of matters at McLean in 1989.

One reason for the outrageous salaries of hospital CEOs seems to be the conviction that only a driven, resolute, competitive leader can do the job. The CEO cannot not be a spectator, not just a distinguished professional whose job is to give dinner speeches. That CEO has to flank herself/himself with a small group of highly able and determined clinical and administrative executives ready to do everything needed: no short cuts, compromises, or window dressing.

"Bring it on" had to trump trying to sidestep the healthcare tsunami. Each well-managed, critical change would, ironically, enliven, not drain, the leadership on the bridge and in the seas of change. These leaders, however capable, can only succeed with a board chair determined to "do well" by "doing good," especially in healthcare. More so, I dare say, in the case of McLean Hospital, where the chair would be accountable for a storied Harvard hospital, and one that clinically served people he or she knew and cared about. A chair, in the case of not-for-profit academic hospitals, like McLean, who would carry the burden and pride of leadership with no salary, but instead was expected to donate generously, not only of their time, but their money as well.

The harmony of the CEO, the executive team, and the board chair is a whole greater than the sum of its parts. They are prepared to engineer what it takes to make it to the moon. That is what differentiates those organizations that last and those that do not.

The consolidation of disparate groups to effect robust and lasting change applied, as well, to the top of the pyramid: those who governed McLean Hospital. Some on the McLean board had their reservations, as did some watching from Beacon Hill in Boston. They were for the CEO, board chair, and others at the organizational summit to engage and ally with.

THE ROAD OF RADICAL CHANGE

History can serve as a remarkable guide on the road of radical change. History identifies the legendary leaders of change. One, of course, is Mahatma Gandhi.

Gandhi helped lead a huge nation to freedom and democracy. He spoke to all of us intent on changing an organization, if not the world. His actions portrayed the pounding and sweeping experience of how a culture is transformed. In stages, too.

As noted in the previous chapter, Gandhi is attributed to have said, "First they ignore you. Then they shame you. Then they fight you. Then you win." Whether he said these words or not, they are consonant with what history attests to as his experience, and to the clarity, wisdom, and irony of a great leader. They have served me many a time, and not only at McLean Hospital.

PS: IS THIS A UNIQUE STORY?

Well in some ways this is a unique story, of course, because of McLean's renown, enduring history, and (can't leave this out) its Harvard imprimatur.

But, principally, no. We don't need a microscope to reveal the troubles that beset hospitals in the 1980s, 1990s, and today (as they did McLean). The ceaseless work of survival is amplified today because of the body blows of COVID to hospital finances and to the most precious of their assets, their doctors, nurses, and a legion of caregivers and caretakers.

Nowadays, too many hospitals are losing money. Many (like me) know what that feels like.

9

THE CORPORATIZATION OF
AMERICAN MEDICINE

An asteroid with great mass and velocity had been headed toward medical care in the United States. Perhaps because healthcare providers could no longer explain, nor could corporate and government purchasers, patients, and the public abide by, the broken, inequitable, and famously unaffordable costs of medical care in this country. And so the asteroid struck, with the consequences upon all of us to this day.

The US spends an estimated $12,318 per person on healthcare, the highest costs among the thirty-plus member countries of the Organization for Economic Cooperation and Development, which serves as a benchmark for economically developed countries.[15] These sky-high costs for Americans are accompanied by a

---

15 The West Health Institute and NORC at the University of Chicago, *Americans' Views of Healthcare Costs, Coverage, and Policy* (NORC at the University of Chicago, 2018).

shorter life expectancy and higher rates of preventable death than in those other member countries.[16]

The public was restive. The National Center for Health Statistics' National Health Interview Survey (2015–2018) found 75 percent of Americans reported not getting value from healthcare, 40 percent saying they skipped a recommended medical test or treatment in the last twelve months due to cost, 32 percent unable to fill a prescription or who took less medication than prescribed because of cost, and over 50 percent of Americans reporting receiving a medical bill they thought was covered by health insurance or where the amount they owed was higher than expected. More than 25 percent had a medical bill from the past twelve months turned over to a collection agency.[17]

Congress could not offer any exit from the mounting dissatisfaction and unaffordability of healthcare, which was no longer a problem just for the poor: Middle-class Americans were now members of a club they had no desire to be in, namely those who were no longer able to afford their healthcare. The medical profession was not going to step in and try to fix this mess. Corporate America (outside of healthcare), while caught in the teeth of these financial problems, knew this was not their primary product or service. They made cars, steel, computers, food, toys, beverages, and the like. They may have wanted a fix, but they were not equipped to provide one. In other words, no one was in charge, and finger-pointing substituted for accountability and action.

History held no hopeful lessons for last-minute solutions to the

16   David C. Radley, Reginald D. Williams II, Munira Z. Gunja, et al. "Americans, No Matter the State They Live In, Die Younger Than People in Many Other Countries," *The Commonwealth Fund* (blog), August 11, 2022, https://www.commonwealthfund.org/blog/2022/americans-no-matter-state-they-live-die-younger-people-many-other-countries.

17   The West Health Institute and NORC, *Americans' Views of Healthcare Costs*.

troubles of medical care, especially of any scale. And nature abhors a vacuum. The mounting miseries with no hope for remediation bred revolution. But the revolution that came, suddenly and forcefully, was not one of reducing waste and corruption, exercising administrative authority to diminish the burdens upon doctors and hospitals, improving quality, reducing avoidable deaths, improving longevity, and so on. Instead, the "solution" was to make medical care a business, first and foremost. This business would be accountable first and foremost to yield profit for its shareholders and investors, not to care for patients like you and me.

A budget-driven ethos and medical practices thus became the new era in America's healthcare. But this form of medical "business" went awry almost immediately, clinically and morally. Requisite profits came to direct the winds of change. Say goodbye to the long-standing era of traditional medicine, which surely needed improvement but not the razing that has happened. A maze of for-profit insurance and healthcare management corporations now dominates healthcare.

Healthcare insurers, managed care organizations (MCOs), self-insured corporations (there are a great many), and state and federal government agencies could no longer afford the ballooning costs of healthcare.

Enough is enough. The "solution" was to drive right through the obstacles and complexities of a troubled healthcare system, and to replace an ethos of patient care with one of profit making. Equity, quality, access, clinical performance measures, and attention to families and professional caregivers (doctors and nurses) would be mercilessly tossed aside. Why take prisoners?

The result has been the radical, rapid, and disruptive corporatization of American medicine now upending our healthcare industry. Fiscal intermediaries (insurers and managed care companies) have become the agents controlling change. In so doing, they have dumped upon caregiving individuals and hospitals whopping, burdensome, and dubious administrative and financial changes, which are doing more harm than good. Administrators, managers, and billing clerks now are everywhere, their numbers are swelling in corporate, for-profit healthcare, as if they were what good medical care needed. They abound, unlike the diminishing workforce of doctors, nurses, and techs, with non-clinical administrative costs and salaries adding more yeast to America's costly cake of medical care, to mix metaphors.

By way of example, once the asteroid's impact had spread across the landmass of American hospitals and doctors, there stood between you and your medical care an army of unknown people at the end of an 800 number. Often called "care managers," these corporate employees, none physicians at first contact, were trained and paid to follow their employer's propriety decision tree (a.k.a. an algorithm), which would determine whether the services requested by a doctor for a patient would be approved or not. Each company had different proprietary rules for their respective algorithms, hence no standardization and thus no way to compare their performances.

There rapidly became many managed care healthcare organizations that would earn big dollars from taking money from what had previously gone to patient care; the business term for this appalling behavior is "medical loss ratio." Each fiscal intermediary has unique review questions and rules for determining approval, also known as payment. *None* are the same, and *none* make publicly available their decision-making programs, including to a patient's doctor. Hospitals were rapidly being upended by their new rulers, many landing flat on their derrières. That was what was predicted for McLean.

WHAT ABOUT THE PATIENTS?

As I've said before, and repeat here, profit, not patients, became the *first and foremost* goal of these corporate titans. Hospital executives were expected to *make money* (certainly not lose it). That was an explicit mandate to the executives of massive insurance companies, ubiquitous MCOs, and their owners and shareholders. But what about the patients?

A vast number of self-insured corporations saw no choice but to engage fiscal intermediaries to staunch their growing healthcare costs. Yet these intermediaries generated additional costs from hiring administrators and billing clerks. In effect, healthcare premiums (what consumers pay to insurers) were heading higher every year, in part to cover the costs of the additional administrative personnel needed to make a profit.

In addition, city and state budgets were getting clobbered by ceaseless annual increases of the cost of their already substantial medical services, especially the costs of Medicaid programs. And while there was no incentive for state government agencies to turn a profit, they did have to cover the explosively increasing costs of their entitlement programs, especially Medicaid.

For those of you unfamiliar with Medicaid, it is a joint state and federal health insurance program that covers one in five people in the US, including elderly individuals and those with disabilities, as well as 40 percent of all children, nationwide.[18] Medicaid costs, nationally, grew 9.2 percent to $734 billion in 2021, or 17 percent of total national healthcare expenditures.[19] A state's Medicaid

18   National Institute of Mental Health, https://www.nimh.nih.gov/health/statistics/
      mental-illness.

19   "NHE Fact Sheet," Centers for Medicare and Medicaid Services, https://www.cms.gov/
      research-statistics-data-and-systems/statistics-trends-and-reports/nationalhealthexpenddata/
      nhe-fact-sheet.

costs—the capital spent to insure Medicaid beneficiaries—are, for the most part, shared by each state with the federal government. The catastrophic devastation by the corporatization tsunami produced a second tidal wave as government agencies added their force by "managing" the care provided by their entitlement programs (especially Medicaid), which meant fewer dollars were paid to providers of clinical services. The state was guaranteed by the MCOs a percentage reduction in annual growth of expenses while MCOs continued to thrive. There were a lot of governors across the nation seeing their Medicaid costs rising and eating into money needed for schools, roads, safety, and the like.

Medical decisions, some small and some a matter of life and death, were no longer, ironically, for doctors of medicine to make. "Managed care" was code for managing costs. The corporatization of healthcare (including Medicaid-paid services) unleashed a power mower, big enough to sit on and raze healthcare in America. It was sent into the fields of medicine to spin its cutting blades over every acre of land that had theretofore been medical healthcare in the US.

For example, many of us are now limited to *eight-minute visits* with our primary care doctor, the consequence of a production line meant to gather sufficient revenues to cover reductions in insurance payments and the grinding administrative costs of getting paid. There also has been a huge loss of trust in doctors and hospitals, I believe, because they lost control of their operations to third parties—namely for-profit corporate healthcare payers and their intermediaries, the MCOs. There became little difference between corporations and government payers.

WHO SUFFERS?

Healthcare has become unaffordable, including the prescription drugs and copays and deductibles that empty your wallet. EPIC and other brain-draining EMRs (electronic medical records) were built for billing and have forced doctors to spend twice as much time on the EMR as on patient care. Many doctors cannot look at you or me in the examining room because they are typing away on their keyboards, feeding the endless fields of an EMR.

Your health and that of your loved ones went into the hands of a machine, with programming you will not see, because it is proprietary. Authorizations (and reauthorizations) for medical care are determined by a computer algorithm used by an insurer or MCO that directs a care manager's decisions. These software programs are designed to assure that the "house" always wins, because that's what business dictates. Proprietary software now controls the provision of medical care, not doctors and hospitals.

These and other fearsome elements of the corporatization of healthcare have rendered patients and families invisible; the computer programs were set to serve their corporate masters—not the patients they were to serve. We become dehumanized, thereby making "saying no" to needed care easier on what conscience may remain in the C-suites of business. It's not unlike the dehumanization of an enemy in war.

All this in the richest country on the planet.

Quickly, in years—not decades—corporate giants came to lord over national healthcare. They were soon ensconced in the driver's seat of what has become ever more an industry. An industry where serving patients and families is *not* its primary purpose, especially in for-profit healthcare, and now joined by state-led Medicaid programs. If hospitals and their systems of care do not turn a profit, or worse, lose money, God forbid. Those leaders in

C-suite medical care seats would soon be on their way to an abattoir for failed executives.

Could some healthcare institutions, hospitals, and doctors adapt to a corporate, business-first culture, and thereby fiscally survive the asteroid without losing their soul? Yes, it's possible, but as this book reveals, it's not easy, brief, or pleasant. Time and toll await those trying to follow their moral and medical compasses.

MENTAL HEALTH SERVICES

Among the medical specialties, psychiatric services have occupied a top tier of corporate strategies meant to underpay and dismantle services for the most common and disabling of mental disorders, which affect over 20 percent of Americans annually. Payment to inpatient psychiatric units pales in comparison to what GI, cardiac, and orthopedic wards are paid; OB-GYN, urology, and dermatology too. Where can a new cardiac catheterization lab be sited? A psych unit is easy prey; it can be closed and its precious space allocated to profitable medical services. In so doing, hospitals turn on themselves and behave like their corporate masters. There is a psychological term for this—"identification with the aggressor"—introduced by Sándor Ferenczi, a contemporary of Sigmund Freud.

The costliest of mental health and substance use services is an inpatient hospital stay. That's where MCOs first (and still do) focused their decimating laser of corporate control—on the medical specialty of psychiatry. They shamelessly deny care or meagerly, if at all, approve small aliquots of reauthorized days. These methods work, if what is sought is money. One visible consequence is diminishing psychiatric services, needed more than ever after the COVID pandemic. Is anyone paying attention? If not, the fight will surely be lost.

THE CORPORATIZATION OF AMERICAN MEDICINE 119

A number of legal cases against MCOs have been won for not using the same medical necessity criteria for psychiatric services as they do for general medical services (a mandate of the Affordable Care Act) with psychiatry at the short end of the stick.

For every Goliath, there is a David. The monstrous MCOs are responsible for the inequities they create and perpetuate, year after year. Providers of services and the subscribers to insurance plans, the Davids, need to continue to use their trove of legal, ethical, and moral slingshots to topple the profit-driven monsters making medical decisions without a medical license.

MCLEAN IN THE CROSSHAIRS

McLean, a renowned Harvard teaching hospital, squarely came into the crosshairs of medical corporatization. Not a good position to occupy, I can assure you. Abide or go fallow. McLean Hospital, where I was chief medical officer for eleven years, serves as a cautionary tale, though one that ends well. But not without radical and disruptive clinical and service changes, which tested the mettle of McLean (as it will other hospitals, doctors too).

Half-hearted clinical changes would not keep McLean alive, to live to regain its clinical prominence and financial stability.

10

AN IATROGENIC DISORDER

Soon after becoming medical director at McLean, I asked my clinical colleagues who was the longest-stay inpatient we had. There seemed no difficulty identifying her; she had been hospitalized for more than 1,000 days—heading toward three years, uninterrupted, on an inpatient unit. Let's call her "Ms. Lasting."

I read her medical record, thick as could be. I spoke with some of her doctors and nurses, and a number of senior clinical chiefs and hospital administrators. I spoke with our business office. She was a single woman in her thirties. Remarkably, unheard of today, a combination of her commercial insurance payment and her (diminishing) family trust account had been fully covering what had accrued to be a huge McLean Hospital bill. Had she improved? Had there been efforts to transition her, with psychiatric rehabilitation and supports, to community-based services? What were her goals? What did *she* want? The answers I obtained were not what I had hoped to hear.

She was not psychotic, but her mood was quite unstable; she was given to bouts of anger and tearfulness, but not mania. She frequently was self-destructive, injuring herself in myriad ways, though none life-threatening. While Ms. Lasting often spoke about wanting to kill herself, she had not acted on that impulse during her extended stay at McLean. She had not befriended any other patients, had limited and contentious therapeutic relationships with doctors, nurses, or aides, and eschewed contact with her family. Her most frequent visitor seemed to be the attorney who was the executor of the family trust.

A host of medications had been tried, as had different psychotherapeutic and supportive therapies. No luck. Different doctors had tried to work with her. A number of them had attempted to help her leave the hospital, which had sent her into a bad tailspin, with more expressions of self-abuse and intent to die. She had defeated every doctor who had tried to have her leave McLean. An essentially permanent hospital stay is the antithesis of recovery.

BEHAVIOR SERVES A PURPOSE

My "aha!" moment came from one fundamental principle that has guided my professional work—namely, that, as a rule, behavior serves a purpose. This principle was one of four "secrets" I described in my 2017 mercifully short book, *Improving Mental Health: Four Secrets in Plain Sight.*[20] The "secrets" were later made into four three-minute videos, which many an audience liked.[21]

The idea that behavior serves a purpose was a big piece in

---

20   Lloyd Sederer, *Improving Mental Health Care: Four Secrets in Plain Sight* (The American Psychiatric Press, 2016).

21   Lloyd Sederer, "Dr. Lloyd: The Four Secrets," Vimeo video, https://vimeo.com/316636397/c8f5e61054.

solving the puzzle of why Ms. Lasting could not get better, no less leave the hospital. What purpose did Ms. Lasting's behavior serve? Her illness was not sufficient explanation for her aversion to leaving the hospital.

My McLean colleagues had been working with the (understandable) premise that this patient wanted to get better, that she wanted to have a life outside the hospital, with sources of support and meaningful activities.

But . . . *what if* her goal was to remain continuously attached to her doctors and the hospital?

ATTACHMENTS

Human attachments have been long studied and widely reported in psychological literature. Attachment theory (see the work of René Spitz, Melanie Klein, D. W. Winnicott, Harry Harlow, and others) posits the ways by which we humans develop our inner emotional attachments, which in turn shape our relationships and behaviors.

The principal styles of attachment have been termed "secure" and "insecure" attachment. Of course, they exist on a continuum. Yet, a prevailing style can be recognized in children—sometimes as early as at one year of age. Each style (or type) will differently shape how that child (and later adult) responds to the challenges we all face with maturation, including the capacity (or not) to be alone, the ability to act with some confidence in relationships (or not), self-expression (or not), and the capability for intimacy with others (or not).

Secure attachments, in adults, are marked by a person's ability to put into perspective disappointments, frustrations, separations, and minor traumas. People with secure attachments are resilient to being hit by the inescapable slings and arrows of our respective lives. They have the capacity to be emotionally close to others and intimate, to permit themselves to turn to others for care and support, and to be responsibly dependable themselves.

Insecure attachments are often seen at an early age and persist into adulthood if there are not experiences to alter them. *Preoccupied/anxious* variants are intently focused on their relationships—and whether they can depend on others. This type of attachment is prone to remain highly connected to and reliant on parents and others who have served as their caregivers. They can seem emotionally starved, desperate for connection, given to acting in dependent, childlike ways, and to turn to desperate, self-destructive efforts to sustain contact with whoever has become their primary support(s).

If Ms. Lasting got better and left the hospital, she would lose her caretakers as well as the support she felt from the hospital, the institution itself. This loss likely would be bearable for a person with secure attachments, but it is often unbearable to a person with deep, persistent, insecure attachments.

This patient's goal was to maintain her relationships with her caregivers and a hospital—*not* to get better. To achieve her goal, she needed to defeat our efforts to help her improve (and be discharged). Remarkably, she defeated those efforts for over 1,000 days. Ms. Lasting's need to thwart recovery, please understand, was not conscious to her, but was, inside, an eight-cylinder psychic engine, which could only be deduced from her behaviors.

Her descents into despair, her cutting and other self-destructive acts, and claims that if she were discharged, she would promptly employ a deadly means of taking her life now made sense. They served the purpose of protecting her from losing all that she had become dependent upon. No doctor had been able to abide with discharging her when she was pronouncing she would kill herself if that happened. Her self-destructive actions, when facing discharge, made that claim carry some heft. She was assigned one doctor, then another, went from one ward to another. She had become the longest-stay patient still in McLean Hospital. The longer she stayed, the more reliant she became. The hospital, ironically, could not help her make a life, other than as a mental patient.

While this case history may be an extreme example, I offer it to underline how remnants of the "old" McLean culture of protracted stays resulted in her not standing out, as she would almost anywhere else. One thousand, five hundred, even one hundred inpatient days are great, outlier data points (with the exception of most state hospitals). One thousand days had not worked and did not speak well of McLean. The goals of a hospital admission are to provide critically needed treatment—and to conclude the care when it is no longer needed.

Difficulty with achieving a safe and responsible hospital discharge calls for a careful review, asking "why?" and revising the treatment plan in response to the "why," not necessarily more time in the hospital. The response to "why" begs attention because lengthy stays carry substantial risk of loss of functioning by a patient, leaving them less able to leave the hospital.

I decided to become Ms. Lasting's doctor, to assume responsibility for her care (I have been told I jump off cliffs)—for her sake *and* to measure up to McLean's new mission to deliver inpatient care briefly, not unendingly. But I said little about my formulation about why no one had succeeded in discharging her. Timing can be everything.

SETTING THE STAGE

Before launching into this Hail Mary scenario, I sought more background. I spoke with the executor of her trust: She still had substantial trust funds, though another year or two at McLean would largely exhaust those, leaving her with little resources to live upon (she was far from being able to work after three years of being fully cared for). Looming, as well, was that her insurer kept saying they were going to deny payment because she no longer met their criteria for continued inpatient care. The loss of insurance payment would more quickly dissipate her financial holdings since the hospital (and doctor) bills then would all be paid from her trust. She was burning through her money and healthcare coverage. Like a plane running out of fuel, she was headed into a nosedive.

I also contacted her family (with her permission), who, though having become distant from her, were prepared to join in on discharge necessities like where to live (not with them), transportation, shopping, and so on once she left the hospital.

Few patients will have the means and support available to them if and when they could bear to leave the hospital.

My conversations with her were at first short because my message evoked all manner of outbursts (including yelling, crying, and asserting I was "heartless"). Still, I had to stay the course I had set because quick psychological fixes may occur in fictional settings like the movies, but seldom do in the world of nonfiction hospitalizations. The hospital itself had become her "illness." No therapy or medication could fix that problem.

In medicine, we have a term for when the doctoring itself is causing the problem: an "iatrogenic disorder." After a number of initial meetings, she threatened to kill herself if I discharged her. I said we both needed for her to leave and stay alive. The day of reckoning, of discharge, could not be indefinitely in the future. I set a discharge date for four weeks later.

Suffice it to say, it was a stormy four weeks. But she had no significantly harmful behaviors. I spoke with her family, with her permission, to give them a timeline that had not existed before.

Mostly, however, when I was with her, I was talking to myself. Ms. Lasting, at those times, had no interest in exploring what I was saying or in what its implications might be; hence she said very little. We basically had no therapeutic exchange because she had yet to gain perspective on her dilemma. Insight that leads to change draws from a need to know why, not from becoming enraged and blaming her doctor.

One step at a time. Behavioral steps, taking action consistent with treatment goals (like spending time off of a hospital ward, searching for an apartment, urging her to connect with old friends) are effective ways for a person to find their emotional footing, so to speak. They are ways to gain confidence in their capacity to function, which had largely disappeared from sight.

Like the Reverend Martin Luther King Jr. once said, "If you can't fly then run, if you can't run then walk, if you can't walk then crawl, but whatever you do you have to keep moving forward."

Discharge Day arrived. Ms. Lasting behaved as if it were the end of the world, her world. The unit staff, nevertheless, helped her pack and be ready for the car that would pick her up. I came to the ward, signed the discharge order, and said goodbye to her. She left quietly—to my surprise.

A BEND IN THE ROAD

But it was not over. Not for her. Maybe that was why she quietly left the unit and got into the car. The beachhead had not yet been breached.

Late the next day, the hospital switchboard (remember those?) rang me to say there was an emergency call from a patient of mine.

I picked up the phone and Ms. Lasting's familiar voice tremulously told me she had been "abducted." She had been held hostage, she stated, not far from the hospital, but had escaped. She wanted to come back into McLean. I did not ask for more details, but did ask if she could get here, and she said yes. I would meet her in the admitting area to review what had happened.

There she was, her clothing creased and dirty, more scratches on her arms. But she had no credible story about what happened— where, how, by whom, and so on. She had fabricated the entire tale so she could be restored to the institutional care she had become reliant on.

I could not admit her, I said to her, repeating my refrain about the hospital having become her illness. I did not confront her about the story she had constructed; that would only cause her pain—and I didn't even know if she believed it or not. But my plan was clear: We would arrange another car (with the suitcases she had brought back to the hospital) and pick up the discharge plan from the day before. And off she went. Another member of her clinical team contacted the family about the delay but not about the fictitious abduction.

She was not my first patient with an iatrogenic illness, which are all too common. Taking responsibility for Ms. Lasting's hospital treatment was in her interest. And it was, as well, in the interests of McLean Hospital. Unnecessary, in fact deleterious, treatment was not good care, to say the least. It also continued to portray hospital care as not worth paying for.

My "boots on the ground" effort with this patient was but one way I would work to change the hospital's long-stay culture. I knew, of course, there would be many more and diverse actions we would take to radically bring McLean into the arena of modern medicine. Every action we took needed to be a statement about our new mission and the model of care we were creating. When

11

WHEN TREATMENT IS TOXIC

As a rule, less is more

A doctor's oath, no incidental matter, is *primum non nocere* (first, do no harm). Ancient Egyptian doctors knew and recorded back in 1700 BC that wounds of various types did best when any debris was removed, were washed gently with water, and covered to prevent infection and foster natural healing. I see their overall approach, some 3,700 years ago, to have been, *as a rule, less is more.*

Fast-forward to the fourteenth century with the invention of guns and their use in that era's ample number of wars. Gunshot wounds were an everyday battlefield consequence. But to treat gunshot wounds, often infected, battlefield surgeons poured boiling oil into the wounds of soldiers who survived being shot. The results were, as you can imagine, disastrous. Did that not eliminate the boiling oil "treatment"? Hardly. In fact, this barbaric practice was sustained for 200 years until, by serendipity, a

French army surgeon ran out of oil. Lacking the "necessary" oil, the surgeon removed any debris, washed the wound with water, and protected it by bandages. It took 200 years for the gentle and simple care of wounds to become the standard once again for treating battlefield wounds.

The less-is-more approach proved far more effective than what had become standard practice. Of course, it should have been obvious that boiling oil is not an effective cleaning tool—just listen to their screams and count the body bags. But what if a doctor doesn't understand the harm to a patient that his or her treatment is inducing? What if the doctor earnestly believes a treatment he or she is prescribing to be safe and effective, when, for example, there are only unwelcome drug effects with no evidence of benefit? What if doctors with good intent are inadvertently causing their patients harm? What if doctors see only what they want to see?

"We don't see things as they are, we see them as we are."[22]

NOT DOING THE RIGHT THING

After a few months on my new job at McLean, I had my "list" of what McLean doctors and other clinical staff were doing that I believed ran contrary to a patient's recovery yet were sustained by prevailing but faulty and dated clinical theories and practices. Doctors, psychiatrists not only surgeons, can believe they are providing the best of care when, instead, inadvertently, they are doing quite the contrary.

Three clinical approaches at McLean were high on my list

---

22   H. M. Tomlinson, *The Gift* (New York: Harper & Brothers, 1931), 148–49.

because, in my view, they are particularly antithetical to recovery from a mental or addictive disorder. These three practices were not going to help our patients, or help McLean be a center of psychiatric excellence.

The first faulty approach was intensive forms of individual and group psychotherapies that could distress and destabilize a vulnerable, psychotically ill, or borderline disordered patient, which were frequently the mental states among seriously ill McLean inpatients.

The second was polypharmacy—the simultaneous use of multiple medications, often of the same class. For example, prescriptions that combined antipsychotic agents like haloperidol, and olanzapine and Thorazine; two mood stabilizers like valproate (Depakote) and lithium at times also with an antipsychotic drug with FDA approval for use in mood disorders, such as aripiprazole (Abilify), olanzapine (Zyprexa), and lurasidone (Latuda). Sedating drugs from different classes of medications, like clonazepam (Klonopin), zolpidem (Ambien), alprazolam (Xanax), or trazodone might be prescribed together; but even at a lower dose than when prescribed singly, this is polypharmacy. It was not uncommon for a patient with a serious and persistent mental illness to be prescribed, daily, eight to twelve different drugs from several classes of psychoactive medications.

Third was the use of restraint and seclusion (R/S), an increasingly antiquated approach that could cause more harm than good. R/S involved immobilizing a person in bed using leather belts attached from the person's limbs to the bed railings, meant to control or prevent harmful behavior.

There were other items on my list. I chose these because of their frequency, potential for psychological toxicity and other forms of harm, and capacity for remediation.

INTENSIVE PSYCHOTHERAPIES

In 1986, Dr. Bob Drake, a good friend and colleague, and I published two sequential papers on the "negative" effects of intensive psychological treatments of schizophrenia.[23] We reported on how intensive psychotherapy (either delivered very frequently, or emotionally confrontative, unstructured, or deeply explorative) can produce overwhelming and unnecessary psychic stimulation in vulnerable patients, thereby inducing psychological regression, including further loss of reality testing and functional capability. In our papers, we used the battlefield practice of healing wounds with boiling oil as a metaphor for doing more than needed with McLean patients, without value and apt to unnecessarily aggravate their open, psychological wounds. This was several years before I landed at McLean.

Drake and I were working in Cambridge, Massachusetts. We both had seen too many occasions where a fragile patient, with the chronic illness of schizophrenia or other psychotic states, was brought to the emergency room in the hospitals where we worked, in an acutely psychotic state. After an extended period of stability—though still with a mental illness dormant or imminent—that was best not perturbed by doctors and other mental health colleagues. We began to wonder about what had toppled a previously stable psyche and life. We knew that could be the loss of a loved one or the loss of a home, a job, a friend, or a pet (dog usually), discontinuing medications, abusing alcohol, cannabis, or other drugs, among other stressors. But we could not account for many of the relapses by these well-known triggers.

---

23   R. E. Drake and L. I. Sederer, "The Adverse Effects of Intensive Treatment of Chronic Schizophrenia," *Comprehensive Psychiatry* 27, no. 4 (July/August 1986), 313–326; R. E. Drake and L. I. Sederer, "Inpatient Psychosocial Treatment of Chronic Schizophrenia: Negative Effects and Current Guidelines," *Hospital and Community Psychiatry* 37, no. 9 (September 1986), 897–901.

If we look in today's rearview mirror, the 1980s (and before) were when psychoanalysis was still the primary treatment for mental conditions, maybe not in rural America, but common in Cambridge, Massachusetts, and other urban areas. Our inquiries revealed that both seasoned doctors and those in psychoanalytic training (principally psychiatrists then, unlike psychologists today) were treating not just professors and pianists but also people living under marginal living conditions, often where psychically vulnerable people with chronic psychotic illnesses were known to drift.

In time, we had a good sample of examples and published our findings in order to alert our colleagues to go gently with seriously ill patients. I don't know how well our "lessons" disseminated and were adopted. But I did see, right off in 1989 when I began at McLean, that psychoanalytic psychotherapy (a near derivative of formal psychoanalysis) was going strong. It was a predominant treatment (in addition to medications) at the hospital.

In addition, private doctors were not prescribing medications or closely interacting with nurses and social workers on day-to-day care. We needed team play, not time-out. We needed to ensure that no boiling oil would be used at McLean, as Drake and I cautioned about. This put intensive psychotherapy with seriously ill patients at the top of my list of potential harms to McLean patients.

The alternative—the gentle, less-is-more approaches—would aim to build practical social and self-care skills, encourage problem-solving, and furnish psychoeducation about the patient's mental illness (substance use too), all at a pace the patient could tolerate. These therapeutic approaches foster improved functioning and moving ahead on a path to recovery in people with serious mental disorders.

Those were the objectives we at McLean needed to pursue. And we did so, over time, in part by creating our psychiatric staff practice, where we would recruit psychiatrists and psychologists whose work would no longer be the long-standing model of private attendings providing psychotherapy (while ward doctors did the lion's share of the work). A model of staff psychiatric employment who were directly responsible for individual patient care was new to the medical staff of this hospital; it would mean having (and paying) McLean doctors as inpatient psychiatrists, who would provide and manage all aspects of a patient's care—including short-term practical and problem-solving therapies, family education and support, medications, and aftercare planning. In other words, we systematically replaced the services previously done by private attendings with a staff model of care. This was a *shift* to what our patients needed, not what doctors at McLean (psychologists too) wanted to do. That took a few years to fully achieve, and we saw recovery sooner and more substantively in our patients served by our new model of acute psychiatric care. This was, I assure you, a major medical culture shift that happened progressively and which has lasted to today.

POLYPHARMACY

Let's start by overhearing this simulated conversation between a doctor and a patient:

> **Dr. Clueless, speaking to his patient:** *Mr. Jones, our clinical staff now thinks you are ready for discharge from the hospital. I know this has been your goal as well. Your social worker will help you connect with outpatient treatment and to maintain your Medicaid insurance.*
>
> *As your doctor, I want to go over the medications I*

have prescribed you, which clearly helped. That means you will need to continue to take them outside of this hospital.

Here's your medication list:

- *Lithium 900 mg twice a day*
- *Depakote 500 mg twice a day*

You will need blood levels on both these medications, which your outpatient doctor (or nurse) will schedule for you. The levels might result in adjusting the dose of either or both drugs.

- *Olanzapine 10 mg three times a day*
- *Seroquel 5 mg upon awakening and at bedtime*
- *Klonopin 2 mg twice a day*
- *Trazodone 50 mg at bedtime*

I want to stress that carefully following this medication plan will help you function and likely keep you out of the hospital.

REALLY?

Okay, let's consider this plan. Mr. Jones has been prescribed two mood stabilizers, each twice daily, from the same class of drugs, perhaps at the same time of day, making for four pills a day. He also has been prescribed two antipsychotic agents, one twice a day and the other three times a day, at different (and frequent) times, for another five pills a day. The patient has been prescribed a tranquilizer (Klonopin) twice a day, so another two pills per day, as well as a sleep medication (trazodone) once a day. That's a total of twelve pills, every day, taken at various times. And it does not include other medications for general medical conditions like asthma, heart disease, hypertension, and diabetes. Mr. Jones "hates" the psychiatric medications because they make him tired and constipated, and they kill his sex drive. They also remind him he has a serious mental illness.

In addition, a day program has been set up for him to attend three times a week, and his sister stops in every once in a while. This means he is alone most of the time—solely responsible for taking all those medications he hates.

It is a stubborn and widespread *fiction* that any patient with a psychotic disorder will take twelve pills a day of numerous sorts of psychiatric medications and do so of their own volition. Remembering the schedule alone is a moon shot. Could you or I? What if we hated taking them? And what if we suffered from the impaired insight and other cognitive deficits frequent in people with severe, persistent mental illness? Wouldn't we then see significant problems with adherence?

Some European countries are using a *polypill*, where several medications are compounded into one pill that treats, for example, heart disease and hypertension while reducing the risk of stroke. Polypills have their proponents and critics—but we need to fully realize that taking one pill, once a day, stands to deliver the highest rates of patient medication adherence. It is a regimen that realistically is most suited to most of the populations on Planet Earth, especially those living in poverty and with poor access to healthcare.

HARM

Polypharmacy also can be financially toxic. These drugs also can be very expensive to hospitals. Not a good burden to shoulder with increasing operating costs when revenues kept falling. A failure to effectively treat someone also means lost time at work, which is not good if a person wants to keep a job, or diminished functioning in a household, not good for families. Lost time also costs the employer, because they are robbed of day-to-day, over time, reliance on a full workforce to run a good business.

Polypharmacy also can be physically toxic. Multiple medications can interact in unknown ways in a patient's body. If more than one medication is added simultaneously and there are adverse effects, then determining the causal agent becomes elusive.

Polypharmacy is toxic in yet another way—namely, when the ostensible need for it has become a Hail Mary, crowding out considerations of non-medication interventions, including cognitive behavioral therapy, social skill development, and what is called cognitive remediation[24] (CR), which is improving the executive functions of the brain (short-term memory, sequencing of activities like what to do in what order, for example, when we wake up and get ready for the day). Because CR generally is done using video games (designed to focus on these and other mental functions), our patients tend to like it, not hate it like they do medications, a big factor in achieving treatment adherence and retention.

Dr. Clueless's singular focus on medications seems to have not considered the vital importance of psychosocial matters, such as the patient's living arrangements and family support (more than what case managers and social workers can possibly deliver).

There also is the ability to pay for medications when insurance requires even modest co-payments. "Rent or pills. Food or pills," we hear from our patients.

---

24   I. Amado and L. I. Sederer, "What Is Cognitive Remediation in Psychiatric Practice and Why Do We Need It?" *Huffington Post*, August 13, 2013, http://www.huffingtonpost.com/ isabelle-amado-md-phd/cognitive-remediation_b_3728023.html.

Too many pills, with too many side effects, that are too costly, and produce the daily shame of facing the gravity of a chronic mental disorder. Those are not a recipe for success, for the patient or the prescribing doctor.

Polypharmacy approaches carry the risk of toxic patient care. *Res ipsa loquitur.* The problems it fosters are enough to imply a form of indifference, if not negligence. During my years at McLean, we were fortunate to have the clinical leadership of its varied specialty programs pick up the mantle of what I liked to call "prudent pharmacology." Diminishing polypharmacy could be done by crisper thinking, not mindlessness. Yet another way by which McLean would excel in our mental health community.

LONG-ACTING MEDICATIONS

I have treated and overseen the care of a great many patients in private and public settings; it is a privilege to do so. I know first-hand that some are so ill, and aggressive too, that there are times complex medication regimens, at high doses, are needed to quiet their agitation and psychosis. But severely ill patients are a small percentage of those we serve, while a *legion* of mentally ill patients are being prescribed more than they need—and can manage. Shorter hospital stays foster polypharmacy because there is pressure to reduce symptoms in order to achieve discharge, and little time for recovery.

One important solution to a person being unable to follow a complex medication regimen is LAI (long-acting, injectable) antipsychotic medications. The duration of an intramuscular shot is weeks to months. But they often are not used. I don't think that's principally because of the patient. The use of LAIs mostly rests with doctors and nurses. We need to ask those clinicians who are not using LAIs, "Why not?" To puzzle about what might change their prescribing practices. Are there specific educational and training approaches as well as practical help with storage and administration that might help many use LAIs, to the benefit of all involved? LAIs are a good alternative to polypharmacy.

GOING TO SCALE

Some years after my time at McLean, in New York State's vast public mental health system, when I was chief medical officer, the use of high doses of multiple, same-class medications was the rule, not the exception. The state hospitals and their clinics exist for those patients who failed to get better with community and general hospital care. My state agency ran twenty-two state hospitals, scores of outpatient clinics, and served a large population of imprisoned men and women with serious mental illnesses. We employed over 500 psychiatrists and general practitioners, who staffed the state's clinical care settings.

CRITICAL THINKING

One approach to prudent prescribing that did not lean on mandates, blame, or shame was to advance critical thinking in the agency's medical culture. Doctors are smart; they needed that to make it through medical school, and they score well on tests and questionnaires. They have the brains to use critical thinking *before* they make a treatment decision. Asking our doctors to critically think before acting was more respectful of them than declaring bureaucratic mandates.

On homemade printed forms, I "asked" our doctors to complete a set of questions too often ignored by a prescriber—for example, was there something in the patient's medication history that could tell us what worked and what did not, and why? What do you (doctor) think can be achieved ("be specific") by adding another medication? *Or* have you considered nonpharmacological, psychosocial interventions, like a case manager or gaining stable, safe housing? Another question asked was if indeed the doctor or team were observing medication toxicity, *not* symptoms of untreated mental illness. The answers to these, and other questions, were not for me or others in the Admin Building; they were for each doctor to more fully exercise her or his brain in the day-to-day clinical work of patient care in a caring and effective hospital, clinic, outreach/crisis team, or forensic ward.

We needed to reach McLean doctors who sincerely believed they were providing the best of care when, instead, they were unknowingly violating their Hippocratic oath. I see this as a supervisory matter because when well-handled there is no shame or blame, instead helping the doctors better care for their patients.

It took tinkering and time to introduce critical thinking, highlight the problems of polypharmacy and its alternatives, and offer thoughtful supervision (not lectures) that could make our prescribing practices better. All informed by science and experience, and with proof of effectiveness from the clinical improvement measures we put in place and used. The result was that patients felt safer and better cared for by the historic McLean Hospital. Something paramount for our clinical colleagues to take pride in.

RESTRAINT AND SECLUSION

Third on my list (though, right up there with the others) was to reduce the restraint and then seclusion of inpatients at risk to harm themselves or others. For a long time, my field has taken its licks for its coercive practices, including commonly using restraints to immobilize a patient for not just safety, but also because of a prevailing view of the "necessity" to control psychiatric inpatients and to sustain control of a ward.

McLean's specialty units for psychotic and mood disorders received acutely ill patients with diagnoses of schizophrenia, schizoaffective disorder (with both symptoms of psychosis and mood disorders); bipolar illness, especially presenting as mania; and severe depressive states with psychosis. The units in these two programs were serving very challenging patients, across this diagnostic spectrum.

The use of the diagnosis of schizoaffective disorder, in particular, grew over my time at McLean. I don't think there was an increased prevalence of this condition in the general population, but, rather, because mood symptoms, many present in people with schizophrenia, were better identified. The clinical value of identifying mood symptoms was that there increasingly were medications for mood instability, especially lithium and Depakote, and then later the second generation of antipsychotic medications, including aripiprazole and olanzapine.

This is a bit of the tail wagging the dog—where a remedy (mood stabilizers here) has the diagnosis align with the drug regimen, rather than vice versa. I have long thought that psychoactive medications do not target a diagnosis, but rather the active symptoms of a disease. When we paid better attention to mood symptoms (the tail) their treatments were wagging the tail of diagnosis.

Still, these units, with greater patient acuity, had the highest rates of restraint and seclusion in the hospital (with restraint of geriatric patients being another matter). We carefully monitored and recorded rates of R/S to meet our accreditation and licensing standards—which were there for good reasons. It was becoming very clear that the coercion and utter control exercised when placing a patient in restraints was psychologically traumatic to the patient. It often became a reason they avoided further psychiatric treatment, lest they be subject to its trauma once again.

Yet, as I listened to ward staff, aides, nurses, and doctors, I repeatedly heard a view that, unless the patients knew staff were in control, there would be all hell to pay. Sadly, correctional facilities hold the same view.

A loud and agitated patient was either going to stop right off or five or six staff would surround and descend upon them, and route the patient to the nearest seclusion room, empty of any furniture except a bed with leather straps attached (or nearby). Then the staff would use their collective strength to put the patient onto the bed, supine (on his or her back), and quickly apply leather restraints to the wrists and ankles (called "four-point restraint"). Many patients fought violently against being tied down. Sometimes the patient would be physically injured, though rarely requiring medical attention because of the skill of our staff.

As soon as the restraint was completed (sometimes with an additional leather strap across the chest), a nurse would administer "chemical restraint" (later termed as an acute treatment) an intramuscular (IM) injection that typically combined haloperidol (Haldol, an antipsychotic agent) with lorazepam (Ativan, a benzodiazepine agent), at times with Benadryl as well. The patient's resistance to the forced, IM medication added another chapter to what for them was a scary event. Other patients on the ward could not help but hear the fracas, adding edginess to the unit's ambient atmosphere.

For many patients, the shot kicked in quickly, putting them into a sedated state. The (initial) battle was then over. But it could emerge again in one to two hours, with the doctor needing to order a second IM injection.

I was not naïve to the use of restraints, having had my residency training and clinical experiences in a government and general hospitals. If I was on duty, I would order the shot. I felt a mixture of relief and regret in the wake of the restraint.

But now I was no longer a resident or junior doctor; I was the medical director of the damn hospital. When visiting units, as I routinely did, I saw many patients strapped to their bed, with a psych aide posted at the door to intervene to ensure the patients' safety from self-harm or compromised respirations; this was called "one-to-one" supervision, and was a requirement of our state, licensing, and accreditation regulations.

I studied McLean's R/S rates, which were not as high as many other hospitals nationally, psychiatric and general, but were far from the low rates attained in some other hospitals. The regular use of—and reliance on—restraint and seclusion was not good enough for the McLean we were rebuilding. I spoke with the clinical directors of the psychosis and the mood disorders program, as well as the clinical director of the geriatric program.

They knew I was bent on reducing restraint and seclusion at McLean and joined me in that effort; bless them. They soon saw the unnecessary, quotidian violence and trauma from R/S. Any reserve on their part was short-lived as we quickly set about creating a continuous quality improvement (CQI) team. And we went from being witnesses to actors in creating a better, more humane McLean. My great aide-de-camp, Dr. Gail Tsimprea, was there adding her great sense of mission and guiding our work to a successful outcome, as she did in so many other ways in the eleven years we worked together. She was fortune shining on me.

There was one metric in our R/S data that I think fueled our successes in reducing McLean's rates of R/S on the units we started with (and soon other McLean specialty units as well).

Our data showed that *more staff than patients* were injured during restraint, some needing time off to recover and a few going on temporary disability.

I could not believe this critical a data point had gone unmined and not minded. So, we launched our CQI team, building support from other clinical directors, senior doctors, and perhaps more so with the fine nursing leadership of McLean, with Linda Flaherty being our director of nursing. We published our findings in our quarterly (at first), public outcomes publication, *McLean Reports*, as we did many other CQI projects.

As I write this chapter, I have before me the fourth issue of *McLean Reports*, spring 1997, featuring the reductions in restraint and seclusion we achieved over four years. The McLean R/S hour rates (the hours spent in R/S) went from 289.6 hours per 1,000 patient days to 189.6 then to 115.2 and at the time point of that report to 75.3. Those are big changes in practice and culture for all of our clinical staff to be proud of.

It's more proof that McLean was rising to its place as one of the best psychiatric hospitals in the country, if not the world. As Margaret Mead said, "Never doubt that a small group of thoughtful, committed citizens can change the world. Indeed, it is the only thing that has."

So concludes the three areas of changing psychiatric practices that were meant to successfully target toxic aspects of our treatment and patient care, however inadvertent or well meaning. We had impacted destabilizing, intensive, evocative psychoanalytic psychotherapy, polypharmacy, and the unfettered use of restraint and seclusion. The tone of our hospital wards quieted; they became more humane, so far fewer patients would have the experience of treatment-related trauma and toxicity. We also were able to achieve shorter lengths of stay because our treatments did not get in the way.

Converts to CQI will understand that the beauty and gains of these projects is that they go on and on and on, and their achievements are owned by clinicians, not hospital administrators.

12

GROWTH, REVENUE, AND COST REDUCTIONS

B y the mid-1980s, McLean Hospital was aging in its ideas and methods, not only its buildings. Everything ages. No extensive analysis was needed to reveal its medically calcified culture. It would take more than words and slogans, or the crash landing of big consulting companies charged with fixing problems about which they know nothing, to save McLean.

But McLean, upon my landing, still had a pulse and a battalion of talented clinicians, teachers, researchers, and administrators, the human ingredients to bear the dizzying effects of disruptive change. Unfortunately, a vocal few cast doubt on how McLean was being outfitted for the twenty-first century. Even some of those who saw the asteroid coming remained anchored in the belief that all was well.

With enough work, innovation, and determination, McLean could become, once again, a contemporary, therapeutically trustworthy, and financially solvent hospital. McLean's recovery had to end its financial hemorrhaging, but many changes in clinical practice would have to precede the balance sheets, which could undermine confidence in the disruptive changes underway.

The most meaningful measures of McLean's success, to my mind, were broadening McLean's specialty expertise, diversifying its patient population, and making it a place you'd want your loved one to go for care. McLean had to become a hospital not only for the rich, notables, and celebrities. It also had to become open and accessible to a broad diversity of patients and families (of color, ethnicity, age, and economic status), representing the real world: *world-class care for the world*, if you will. It would also have to be experienced as the therapeutic real deal by those who would seek our help as well as our colleagues locally and nationally.

Only culture change and growth could achieve these aims with lasting success.

CULTURAL SOLUTIONS

The largest changes we'd had to make at McLean involved modernizing its existing clinical model to that of acute, short-term inpatient care, with a growth in services and revenues, cost reductions too. We started here:

"COME ON IN"

Keeping a hotel solvent requires keeping its rooms full. So it is for a hospital, where it means to fill its clinical beds. You can't fill those beds without admissions keeping up with discharges.

As I mentioned earlier, McLean's reputation in the Boston area was that it was impossible to get a patient into the hospital. I was very aware of how difficult gaining admission could be since I had worked in the departments of psychiatry at Massachusetts General Hospital, Mount Auburn, and Cambridge Hospital (now the Cambridge Health Alliance). Clinicians in the emergency rooms or outpatient clinics of these hospitals and many other hospitals, including those outside the Harvard orbit, had generally stopped trying. Or if admission were possible, it would require overcoming way too many hoops, including: proving your patient did not have an acute medical illness (by medical exam and sometimes lab studies); the exclusion of patients in alcohol and drug withdrawal with an active substance abuse disorder; a reluctance to accept patients who were agitated or might become assaultive; no adults on Medicaid; and the sine qua non, insurance approval for admission.

It principally became my job—with the support of McLean colleagues with professional connections to area ERs, psychiatric, and geropsychiatry services—to turn the view of "why bother" to "come on in." That meant rapid, no hassle admissions to McLean, which required changes at McLean that would have sources of admission discover a very different experience when calling, and, no less importantly, our clinical staff feeling that they had the skills and resources needed to accept who and what might be coming.

First, the habits that constipated admission were undone, the bottomless queries that gave the message "go away." We worked with the McLean admissions and business offices so we could abide by, more or less, "just say yes." Not by evolution; there was no time for that. Not quite Nike saying, "Just do it," but close.

Second was reaching out to the doctors and nurses in area ERs to assure them McLean would say yes, unlike the experiences they had had. That does not happen by memo. That also does not happen by phone. That happens by what are known as "high-touch" encounters, meaning face to face. My increasingly old Subaru and I went to the various Boston ERs and departments, universities too. I talked with doctors, nurses, and social workers promising a very different experience if they called McLean for admission. My words would be empty if that did not happen. But it did, thanks to the collective efforts of McLean's Admission Office, the residents and fellows who primarily staffed the hospital during peak admission times (4:00 p.m. to midnight), and senior and supervising psychiatrists, their clinical anchors.

This "door-to-door sales approach" worked. Not overnight but within months. And extended over the course of several years, McLean admissions went from 1,800 a year to over 4,000. "Come on in" became McLean's mantra. However, to do so successfully meant a number of essential clinical changes at McLean, described in the following sections.

COMMUNITY-BASED CARE

McLean had to bring an end to being the isolated "asylum" on the hill. Especially if we were to serve people living in poverty or of color, with limited financial resources, and whose families would be dependent on virtually nonexistent public transportation to the hospital.

Clinical services for children and adolescents (C/A) were our initial and major step toward offering community-based services. We closed the Hall Mercer Program, the inpatient C/A service on the McLean campus, set a bit downhill and facing the Admin Building. It looked like a bunker, true to the school of brutalist architecture, a style fashioned by Le Corbusier in the mid-twentieth century. Neither the outside nor inside was a warm and comforting setting for acutely ill children and their families. And it was by then in violation of countless licensing codes.

The C/A service, like adult inpatient care, had for years operated on an unproven, long-term inpatient care model, not very mindful of separating children from their families. Not that some seriously ill youth don't need long-term care, but whenever possible, it is best done in community settings, rather than in an "otherworldly" hospital, inaccessible to families and others central to the treatment of children with a mental disorder. Moreover, most of the children we were admitting to the McLean campus were from inner-city Boston-area neighborhoods, principally on Medicaid, the shared state/federal health insurance program for youth and those living in poverty. Belmont was not the world these kids or their families knew.

Dr. Phil Levendusky established an affiliation with Boston's Franciscan Children's Hospital. We moved the McLean C/A program there. It was way more convenient for families (and many staff) and more financially sustainable than its former campus-based service. This major off-campus service was a critical milestone for McLean Hospital. We were getting out of our own gates and taking a major step up the mountain we were climbing.

We continued to deliver inpatient (and residential) C/A services on campus as well, moving them to the Codman Building, old but not brutalist. There was, and is today, a paucity of intensive care services for seriously emotionally disturbed children and adolescents. McLean had expanded its C/A program with both community-based and on-campus services. There was no shortage of referrals.

DIVERSIFYING AND EXPANDING THE MCLEAN PORTFOLIO OF CLINICAL SERVICES

Upon my arrival, McLean was providing inpatient psychiatric services, little more, which would shrink to half of its operating beds in the years ahead. We had to build ourselves out of the Valley of Inpatient Services to fashion a viable future for the hospital.

This principally fell to Levendusky. He was an unparalleled composite of clinician, department head, teacher, and entrepreneur. Warm, funny, humble, and determined, he warrants a garland for building and diversifying the McLean clinical portfolio. Today the over forty service programs he fashioned continue to thrive and account for a crucial component of the margin needed to help support inpatient, training, and research costs at the hospital.

HOSPITAL OUTPATIENT SERVICES

When I landed at McLean in 1989, there was but one outpatient clinic: the training clinic for residents and psychology trainees. All other outpatient care was delivered privately on campus and in area hospitals, clinics, and the (overloaded) public mental health services.

In but a few years, each of McLean's specialty divisions opened an outpatient service. McLean psychiatry and psychology faculty (as well as neurology and internal medicine) offered specialty outpatient care as part of a continuum of services distinctive to its divisions of mood and anxiety disorders, substance use disorders, geriatric, trauma, bipolar and psychotic illnesses, and child and adolescent programs, to name some. The pace was fierce: We went from one to about a dozen outpatient clinics over a few years.

From 1989 to 1993, McLean's annual, outpatient visits grew from about near to 39,000 to over 55,000 and were on the increase. Our new staff model of care (more later) I had cooked up with a lot of help was working, bringing a new culture of comprehensive, staff-based services, instrumental to McLean leaving the past behind.

RESIDENTIAL PROGRAMS

When I came to McLean, there was one residential program, a "tony" brownstone in Boston's Back Bay, Berkeley House. By 1994, we were operating a growing fleet of residential programs, off and on the McLean campus.

Some of the residences were part of a specialty program. The Hill and Waverley programs were part of the Mood and Anxiety Program (with Dr. Anthony Rothschild as clinical director). Waverley Oaks, a small cottage near the entrance to McLean, provided residential care for people with substance use disorders, as did Appleton with its CBT-focused treatment (with Roger Weiss, MD, its clinical director). The Bowditch Building, legendary in the past at McLean since it was where the most ill and potentially violent patients had been hospitalized, became a women's residential program. Hope Cottage, nestled in the "green bowl" at the center of the campus, provided residential care for the Bipolar and Psychotic Disorders Program (with Mauricio Tohen, MD, PhD, as its clinical director), as did the Upham Building.

Woodland House became another off-campus residential program, as well as Ledge Cottage. There were others to come, off and on the McLean campus.

McLean had over forty buildings on its campus, some of which were repurposed to be residences (and partial hospital programs). No more downsizing, only growth could save McLean. Moreover, new residential programs were needed to meet the mental healthcare needs of those with serious mental illnesses—and to move away from a reliance on inpatient treatment by a less intense level of care that was safe and effective.

We redesigned buildings, fashioned programs, and dedicated professional staff to these services as fast as we could.

THE PAVILION

As part of our goal of increasing programs at McLean, we opened an exclusive residential program, which we located on the campus in Wyman House, quietly aside of the hubbub of an active hospital, yet still on the hospital campus. The Pavilion offered out-of-pocket clinical services, wrapped in a charming home environment and the amenities of a good hotel. McLean's expertise and reputation attracted patients (or their families) with the financial means to eschew insurance payments, to pay "out of pocket."

The amenities included single, handsome rooms, finer cuisine than offered by the hospital's food vendor and cafeteria, and TVs (no internet back then) but not turndown housekeeping. The privacy this program delivered counted a lot, particularly for those patients who were in the public eye. Most important to its success, however, was the psychiatric (and substance disorder) diagnosis and treatment provided by McLean professional staff, many recognized experts throughout the country or becoming so under the supervision of McLean's senior, supervisory, clinical directors.

Some patients came to the Pavilion for a week or two of intensive evaluation, and perhaps also to start the treatment plan they would follow upon discharge.

We advertised the program in the back section of *The New Yorker*, a magazine that was the right fit for this program. The Pavilion continues to draw patients, over twenty years later. It too helps offset the financial losses that attend inpatient treatment, as well as professional training and research, core to the mission of the hospital.

PARTIAL HOSPITAL PROGRAMS (PHPS)

While a certain percentage of patients need and benefit from intensive care—that need not be inpatient treatment. It could be daytime treatment, without night services. Those usually operate Monday to Friday, half and full days, with the patients residing elsewhere. Some patients are with their families or independent, some being served in community care programs, some in foster care, and some living in McLean-based residential programs.

PHPs provide intensive individual and group therapies, skill-building services (rehabilitation), and psychiatric care. They are licensed to prescribe medications. A robust amount of care is delivered in the course of the day, after which the patient then leaves to reside elsewhere, which is more normalizing than remaining, for example, unnecessarily on a locked inpatient unit.

Medicare and Medicaid funding were at the core of the growth of McLean's PHPs. These payers were also evidence that McLean was attending to the needs of the elderly and disabled (Medicare) and those living in poverty or children (Medicaid). No more only the rich and celebrated.

By fiscal year 1994, McLean was operating, annually, over 43,000 partial hospital "days," an increase from the fewer than 10,000 days that had existed in 1990. By fiscal year 1999, partial hospital days were nearing 60,000 annually. You can imagine the pace we were setting to save McLean Hospital.

But by 1997, the McLean bottom line still was (slightly) in the red, less than $1 million annually. We did not enter the black until 1998. It takes years to pull a hospital out of a death spiral, especially with escalating healthcare costs for workforce, pharmacy, and operating expenses. But we clearly were on the right trajectory; we were beginning to see the sky as we climbed out of a dark hole.

CLINICAL COST REDUCTIONS

We also had to think differently about how we spent money. The big change here was finding ways of reducing costs that, of course, would not adversely affect our patients.

McLean Hospital operated its own certified pharmacy to serve hospital inpatients. Outpatient prescriptions were filled by patients or their families at community-based pharmacies like large chain and independent pharmacies operating throughout the state of Massachusetts or where the patient lived.

There were two ways by which pharmacy costs were steadily reduced. The first was by dint of doctors changing their clinical practices. The second was from the reduced drug costs of generic medications as the brands went off patent, and competition among the generics drove prices down, fortuitously enabling prudent lower-cost pharmacy purchasing.

How did clinical practice changes contribute to the hospital's operating costs? Polypharmacy (see my earlier discussion of this practice) has long been a problem in psychiatry. This was not from doctors trying to build up business for the pharma companies. Instead, it largely was risk avoidance: When a patient is not adequately responding to a given medication, another of the same class may be added, without discontinuing the first medication. This is because of concern that the patient might decompensate, become more symptomatic and less functional, a concern often shared by the patient's family, if not the patient themself.

Without any mandate from above, but with the support of

those who doctors reported to (including me), our prescribing doctors (nurses did not have prescribing privileges at that time) and their colleagues saw that some patients were able to do as well—or better—on fewer medications. Not to reduce costs, though it did that, but to reduce the cumulative side effects from polypharmacy, which helped improve adherence (patients hated the medications less) and which made for more plausible regimens upon discharge.

Another area of cost reduction where my office contributed to was regarding clinical per diem cost reductions, that is, diagnostic testing. When I landed, there was no evident attention to the costs to the hospital of imaging and laboratory testing. McLean had (still has) state-of-the-art brain imaging machines (first CT scans and then MRIs). Why not get a noninvasive brain scan on every patient? Because it is unnecessary and too often leads to incidental findings that prove to be of no use clinically but can lead to more imaging to prove that they are immaterial to the patient's psychiatric condition. Even when a hospital "owns" brain imaging technology, unnecessary scans cost money since there would be no insurance payment for them. The use of McLean's clinical imaging dropped, as did prescribing of multiple medications. Fortunately, the use of brain imaging became (still is) a major research area for the hospital, bringing in research grants and revenue.

We can—and we did—play a similar tune for laboratory testing. "As a rule, less is more" because what emerges from prudent lab testing is clinically useful, not more "noise" about the patient's clinical condition. It saves money too.

PERSONNEL SOLUTIONS

The professional staff, physicians and psychologists, at McLean were a great asset, but not all of them.

As we grew we brought on new staff, selected for their ability to provide superlative and contemporary clinical services. The "laggards" were outnumbered and their role as inpatient psychotherapists was not germane to our model of acute care, leading to reductions of staff by those who moved on. A Medicare regulatory requirement (inurement, discussed earlier) led to no more free offices, which accounted for time for a migration off the McLean campus by many clinical faculty. In other words, personnel changes to support a renewed McLean crowded out those no longer instrumental to the hospital's services. Without roles or benefits (i.e., offices and patients), the exit of attendings from the Higginson Building happened (more or less) without a brouhaha.

As admissions escalated, our outpatient, residential, and partial hospital services expanded, research blossomed, as did the McLean professional staff. Nurses, aides, psychiatrists, psychologists, social workers, rehabilitation staff, and research scientists grew in number to accommodate the ever-increasing clinical demands and federal research grants.

Linda Flaherty, McLean's chief nursing officer, was instrumental in navigating and managing much of the interpersonal and professional relationships that were (still are) at the core of the hospital's ability to attract the excellence needed in its professional staff to deliver safe and effective care.

CREATING THE MCLEAN PROFESSIONAL STAFF PRACTICE

McLean needed and established a Staff Practice, an organization of clinicians paid by the hospital to treat McLean patients. We would not require them (as was then happening in many medical centers, even more so today) to enroll their private patients in the hospital's practice plan. Eschewing the requirement of mandating hospital doctors to migrate their private patients to the hospital's outpatient services was welcome: It would help recruit terrific doctors, as well as retain many of our experienced McLean clinicians.

Over time, about 200 psychiatrists and psychologists joined the Staff Practice. It was a partnership that worked well for them and the hospital. And it was essential to the growth of the clinical care that has McLean going to this day.

CLINICAL MANAGEMENT SOLUTIONS

To meet the increasing medical and neurological needs of an increasingly complex, diagnostically co-occurring patient population who suffered both medical and psychiatric disorders, we created new programs and new departments to better support existing and new personnel to flourish, to provide the best of care. Two notable new departments were medicine and neurology.

The McLean Department of Medicine

A McLean Department of Medicine had never existed (in modern times at least). We recruited the highly able and affable Arthur Siegel, MD, to lead this new department, charged with identifying and serving patients with co-occurring medical conditions in the Admissions Unit and throughout the hospital (e.g., heart disease and hypertension, obstructive airway and other lung diseases, diabetes, gastro-intestinal and autoimmune conditions, the list goes on). Comfort with medical illnesses in Admissions and throughout the hospital grew and allowed McLean to become more of the acute care hospital we envisioned.

When I thought I had a new medical symptom, I often went to talk with Dr. Siegel before I turned to my primary care doctor, I trusted him. He continues to head the Department of Medicine at McLean and expand its services.

The Department of Behavioral Neurology

Behavioral Neurology was still a nascent but vital element in understanding and treating diseases of the brain, especially those known to present behaviorally—including seizure disorders, impairments in memory and concentration, dementing disorders, aggression, and Parkinson's disease, to name a few.

Bruce Price, MD, was a young behavioral neurologist in Boston whom we were proud to recruit. He could be mistaken for a Hollywood leading man: tall, handsome, and gracious, though those attributes were not requisite in his job description. He both expanded the clinical horizons of McLean and developed working relationships with a number of Boston hospitals. He too continues to lead McLean's Department of Behavioral Neurology and has extended his work to cofound a Center for Law, Brain, and Behavior in Boston.

REDUCING OPERATING COSTS

Finally, in addition to the cultural change of thinking about costs differently (e.g., prescribing practices, laboratory and other diagnostics, and pharmacy noted previously), we needed management solutions that would reduce the cost of operations. From its start, the Mirin administration assiduously worked to lower its costs. A dollar saved means one dollar less to earn, a reality that served McLean well. While our entire leadership team was involved, this work was particularly led by Michele Gougeon (EVP/COO) and David LaGasse (CFO).

But there was no escaping our self-determined mandate that the costs of clinical care (independent of overhead) would not be adversely affected. Patients first. After all, we were a hospital.

Operating a campus over one hundred years old, with some buildings close to that vintage, is very expensive. Power, water, facility operations and renovation, maintenance, groundskeeping, the motor pool, and so on were progressively contracted out to vendors. This was hard on those who had been hospital nonprofessional staff, some multigenerational workers from nearby towns. Yet our priority was to cover the costs of clinical services, our core mission, even if that meant having to contract and outsource other services.

Security, however, including officers dedicated to patient and staff safety, remained as McLean employees.

Few operational costs went unexamined and went untouched over time. But since my turf was clinical, I would not do justice more than providing the high points of cost reductions that helped keep McLean Hospital alive.

Nonclinical Revenue

McLean had a few sources of revenue outside the expected clinical sources, which helped offset clinical, research, and training costs, changing the way we spent and earned our nonclinical expenses and assets.

Real Estate

Because McLean sat on 246 acres of land in prosperous Belmont, Massachusetts, a piece of land was sold to developers, who built high-end town houses that were in demand. McLean was able to increase its cash reserves from the sale of the property, adding needed revenue during the dark times of McLean's financial woes.

Benefactors

Notably, McLean has had benefactors going back to the nineteenth century, families wanting to give back for the care their loved ones received. Foundations as well. Together, families and foundations, during my time at McLean and uninterrupted since then, contributed substantially to keeping McLean alive: to enabling investment in the growth of specialty programs and mitigating financial losses until we could turn the hospital around. Often anonymous to outsiders, those in the Admin Building knew many of the major benefactors, and perennially were grateful to them. Dr. Shervert Frazier, upon his return to McLean, served as an invaluable liaison to our donor community.

"Development," as fundraising often is called, was instrumental in the hospital's capital campaigns to modernize its buildings, as well as contributing to funding new clinical programs and innovative research.

THE MCLEAN CAMPUS: AN INVALUABLE ASSET

The legendary landscape architect Frederick Law Olmsted ironically lived out the final five years of his life at McLean Hospital, whose design and landscape he helped create in the late nineteenth century with his business partner, Calvert Vaux. Olmsted had developed progressive dementia (today more commonly known as Alzheimer's disease). His sons placed him in a residential facility on the grounds of the hospital.

Upon entering my office at McLean and looking to the wall to your left, you would see an original Olmsted line drawing of the central campus area, showing circular paths and a number of discrete buildings set in the central core of the grounds. I had found it in the McLean archives, where its neglect had not done it harm. I had it framed and displayed it on a wall in my office in the Admin Building. It felt like a talisman. Security fitted it with an alarm on the back lest anyone tamper with or try to take it (including me).

Olmsted and Vaux's firm designed one hundred public parks and recreation grounds, twice as many for private estates, in addition to scores of residential communities and campuses for academic institutions. Their work (individually and as a pair) included Central and Prospect Parks (New York City), the US Capitol, Elizabeth Park (Hartford, Connecticut), the Arnold Arboretum and the Emerald Necklace (Boston, Massachusetts), the Biltmore Estate (North Carolina), and the grounds for Cornell University, Yale, Wellesley College, Smith College, and Trinity College, to name some of the more prominent of their creations.

Olmsted also was prolific in his landscape work for what then were considered asylums. These included McLean Hospital, Buffalo State Asylum for the Insane (its original name, now Buffalo Psychiatric Center), the Hartford Retreat (later the Institute of Living), the Bloomingdale Insane Asylum (now New York-Presbyterian Westchester Behavioral Health Center in White Plains, New York), and the Sheppard Asylum (now the Sheppard and Enoch Pratt Hospital in Baltimore, Maryland). All were stately havens usually with substantial grounds. McLean was second only to Boston's Arnold Arboretum in its collection of decorative trees.

Olmsted's fame was no protection for his mental instability. Mental disorders spare no sex, age, race, and socioeconomic status. Olmsted was known for his periods of great creativity and output, and for periods of low moods and little productivity. Some consider him to have suffered from bipolar disorder (manic-depressive illness). To my knowledge, this (presumed) illness was not why he entered and remained at McLean—until his death. Only when dementia rendered him incapable of work and self-care did his family turn to McLean for asylum, to help shelter him from the psychic darkness and pain of dementia.

But his contribution of creating a world-class park on which a hospital sat should be heralded. The land was coveted by many worthy and dubious organizations. An extraordinary asset like the McLean property surely drew patients and families seeking care. The McLean campus stood as an icon that distinguished (and valued) the hospital, adding to our resolve to save McLean.

LAST WORDS

That's more or less how we did it, lacking volumes of detail. No way was McLean going to fail; that was contrary to our raison d'être.

The vast and continuously expanding portfolio of programs, a new model of acute care with its Staff Practice, clinical and non-clinical revenues, and a boom in research not only ended McLean's nosedive, but also became the underpinnings of its success—to this day, more than twenty years later. I suppose that's called enduring success—Jim Collins's "built to last."[25] For the singular goal of rebuilding a storied hospital that, would again, be dedicated to serving those in need by delivering essential and beneficial clinical care, training the clinicians of the future, and advancing the science of the brain and the mind.

That's no humbug.

---

25   Collins, *Built to Last*.

13

COUNTING WHAT COUNTS

After several months on my new job, I announced at my monthly meeting of the hospital's division chiefs and senior doctors that we were going to have a "report card." Admittedly, that was a bit out of the blue; it was nowhere to be found on the agenda.

Caught up in my own idea, an innovation for McLean and our field, I added that it would be a public document: not just for the clinical staff but for our board *and* our local and national patient and professional communities as well. We would publish this quarterly performance report about how McLean was doing, not financially or in research but with a singular focus on clinical care.

You may wonder why I didn't plan, no less use, a better approach to introducing what would be considered a radical change than by surprise? My boss, Steven Mirin, was by then fond of telling me that even when I appeared to know the right thing to do, others might not, and of course might not agree. My "wise-guy," unexpected declaration was not my finest moment in advancing change, even if on target.

None of us is keen to have our performance measured, in this case tagged to the names of the respective clinical service chiefs and their programs (but not individual doctors) and made public knowledge. Mind you, this was thirty years ago. While clinical quality measurement and reporting (and improvement) today has become a standard of good practice, it still is an exercise in pulling teeth. And when I began at McLean, no psychiatric program had developed or even implemented a meaningful, actionable, and verifiable "report card" on clinical care and outcomes, as well as the patient's experience of care, which is different from satisfaction. That would be called innovation. What we soon called *McLean Reports* was how McLean would distinguish itself: with proof of clinical excellence that had so far defied adoption in psychiatric services.

Were McLean patients, in their own judgment, better or worse or not changed at all by the services they had received? We would answer that question in the hospital's diverse array of programs by monitoring and assessing the reports of their patients. Self-reports today have become more common, but at that time one question for us to answer was, why did we not turn to existing standardized rating scales completed by the clinicians providing care, or trained research assistants? Principally for two reasons: First, we wanted to show, not just say; we wanted our patients to tell us if their treatment worked and what it was like to be a patient at McLean Hospital. We reported their comments anonymously and not individually to protect their privacy. Second, we had an overextended staff of doctors and nurses for whom even a brief assessment interview could feel like the straw that would break their backs. Our implementation of *McLean Reports* would not have our professional staff put a pen to paper—our patients would do that (with their encouragement and support to complete the two assessments we were seeking).

My profession owes patients, families, payers, and regulators quantitative measures of symptoms and functioning, actual metrics, numbers, not vague statements, to guide our work and achieve better results. It's no different from financial data reporting or, even better, how your primary care doctor measures your blood pressure, lipids, and HgA1C (glucose levels over time). I was appealing to my colleagues for us to "do the right thing," namely measure and report on our work—on quality, outcomes, and patient experiences at Harvard's storied psychiatric hospital. What better time to do so than when we were in the process of re-creating McLean? Not bits and pieces but close to the kitchen sink of change.

Admittedly I had considered some measurement tools when I declared that McLean would have a report card. I had not talked about it with my boss, or my executive team colleagues. Don't start the way I did but do proceed with whatever innovations you can bring to the treatment of mental and addiction disorders.

McLean clinical and moral compasses to guide a dedicated group of professionals intent on continuously improving patient care, was a privilege that must be earned, again and again. That was what I should have said when I made my surely disruptive announcement. Yet the idea quickly gained traction. It helps to have very smart, experienced clinical leaders—many who also are accomplished researchers, where measurement is king (or queen). That day launched, however graceless, McLean's innovative and unique quality mission, one that would distinguish the hospital, then and on to today.

The looks around the room after my report card declaration would have been precious to record. A few of the clinical directors

saved me by asking really good questions, putting me on the spot
to explain why and how we would go about publicly reporting on
how McLean was doing. Once the plan was out of the bag, Mirin
liked the idea, if I could pull it off, of course.

I had yet to learn and employ the practice of never leaving your boss uninformed when you have bad news or intend
to launch significant changes. Mirin was the forgiving type,
when he thought an action was right, feasible too. I had to learn
this lesson again, in a compelling way, when I went to work in
Michael Bloomberg's first-term mayoral administration, as New
York City mental health commissioner. The mayor's then chief of
staff made that plain to me, etching the practice of no surprises
with your boss into my SOP (standard operating procedure).
Then he would consider my "big" ideas for a number of agency
mental health and addiction programs.

In my mind, I still go back to that Rubicon meeting where
we committed to delivering scientifically based treatment matched
with the proof that we were getting it right, again and again: that
we were living up to the level of care we aspired to deliver. The
results we reported would not shame McLean, even when some
needed improvement. We would be proud, I thought, and that
proved to be the case.

THREE DOMAINS OF PERFORMANCE

We would assess three domains of performance important to our
patients and their loved ones. By using quantitative measures,
sensitive to change, in each domain (see the following), we could
improve actual patient care and their experience of their treatment
at McLean. And we would record the results of the fourteen days
we were aiming for as our average length of stay.

We could stand on the shoulders of McLean's Services Research group, led by Barbara Dickey, PhD, and Susan Eisen, PhD. They had the intellectual and psychometric capital called for to implement an audacious performance-based, clinical measurement system for McLean Hospital.

McLean's Services Research group was there before I arrived. Services Research includes studying (1) the provision of existing care, called process review; namely, asking if we actually did what we were purporting to do, and (2) patient clinical symptoms and functioning; the outcomes of their treatment, aimed to find opportunities for always improving psychiatric care. To do its work, Services Research used as its tools meaningful, proven, and quantitative measurement instruments sensitive to change, even in two weeks. We were entering, more so creating, the dawning field of psychiatric (and addiction) quality improvement.

I learned so much from these two brilliant, way ahead of their time, research psychologists, Dickey and Eisen. They were my "ace up the sleeve," when calling for a huge change in McLean's culture of care.

I had found gold in the McLean Services Research group, a stone's throw from my office in the Admin Building. What's more, they reported to the medical director (me), though that is usually not enough to succeed at introducing the magnitude of innovation we sought.

Dickey and Eisen already had begun to develop the measurement tools we would employ. McLean would "count what counted." We would introduce quantitative, performance data for clinical services and patient care by using their two psychometrically (scientifically) proven measurement instruments. These were the BASIS-32 and the PoC, both sensitive to change in as few as the fourteen inpatient days we would come to average.

Making the hospital effective and humane for patients and families could be done, not by boasting but with proof, reliable evidence of the effectiveness of our clinical services. To my knowledge, I don't think there was, at that time, another psychiatric hospital providing the caliber of performance measurement we were introducing.

Our public reports (*McLean Reports*) on the hospital's performance would derive from three data sources.

The first was *administrative data*, especially about patient care: the type of data that reveals the good, the bad, and the ugly of hospital services. We already were collecting much of this data to meet regulatory, accreditation, and licensing requirements. Our administrative data points included average and median length of stays, rates of medication errors and adverse (harmful) treatment events, rates of unexpected transfers to other hospitals, especially for acute medical/surgical treatment, and rates of seclusion and restraint, typically a traumatic experience for patients, often leaving them averse to seeking further psychiatric hospital care. Moreover, staff injuries warranted reporting because they were a common consequence of putting a frightened (thus potentially aggressive) patient into restraints. We also reported on our rates of readmission (within thirty days, as a rule).

There were other administrative data points, but you get the picture. Every one of these metrics lend themselves to clear reporting on graphs and are inescapable evidence of our performance. This information was included in the *McLean Reports*. Everything would be in the public record, always with patient privacy.

The second was *patient outcomes*, which were innovative, no longer by anecdote or surveys. Reporting on outcomes, using scientifically demonstrated, patient-completed tools, meant disclosing the views of those we served, about the mental health and addiction services they received. Outcome measures are the holy grail of all of medicine: They are not assessing what was done to and for patients (process measures), but rather the clinical results patients achieved while under our care. McLean would ask patients to tell us, confidentially, their ratings on symptoms and functioning upon admission and at discharge (from inpatient services at first, then for outpatient care as well).

The clinical rating instrument we used was the BASIS-32 (more a bit later). This was a Likert-like scale of the degree of difficulty (severity) patients experienced about their symptoms and daily functioning—in school, work, and relationships. This was thirty years ago! We stood to break new ground by measuring and thereby determining if we were indeed improving the quality of the lives of those we served, by the psychiatric services we delivered.

The third was what we soon called the *perceptions of care* (PoC). It was common, still is, for hospitals to administer patient satisfaction surveys. We would do better than that: We would query, with the PoC instrument, the actual experiences of patients—their self-report—about McLean staff and the treatment they received. The PoC, too, could be quantitatively measured and presented in graphic form, to better understand the information we had collected—and to use it to inform and direct our quality improvement efforts.

Asking patients to speak for themselves was not in vogue at that time. To double down on an earlier comment, it was critical to not add more paperwork to the workload of doctors and nurses, since every piece of paperwork is time away from direct patient care.

THE BASIS-32

With thirty-two questions, the BASIS-32 (the Behavioral and Symptom Identification Scale) was developed and tested by McLean's Services Research Department. This scale allowed

McLean to query patients about their self-reported difficulties in five domains apt to be meaningful to them:

- Relation to self/others
- Daily living skills
- Depression/anxiety
- Impulsive/addictive
- Psychosis

The BASIS-32 uses a Likert-like scale, a simple gradient of checkboxes of the respondent's perceived degree of difficulty in each domain—with ratings of 0 to 4. Their responses give us (and them) ratings of how McLean, or any other setting that used it, was measuring up, or not, so to speak. It was a spotlight on our work, closer to the experiences of those we served. Not as an exception but an addition to the opinions held by McLean's doctors, nurses, and other hospital professional staff.

If this "emperor" of a Harvard teaching hospital was not wearing clothes, we would be laid bare about our performance, according to the opinions of those we served. All the BASIS-32 outcome data would be publicly reported (as mentioned above) without identifying any specific patient or specific inpatient service—though, often, the latter could be inferred. Those who would see the results would be the hospital staff, its governance and accrediting bodies, and the general public. To assure patients that their scores, their opinions, would not be individually seen by their direct caregivers (the doctors and nurses who held significant power over them in the hospital), we collected the initial report on the Admissions Unit we had established, and the patient completed the follow-up report at discharge from their inpatient unit.

The completed forms were put—by our patients—into a sealed envelope, which was delivered to our Services Research group.

In addition to the BASIS-32 (for age fourteen and older), McLean introduced the PoC; both instruments were developed and rigorously proven to measure what they purported to do by two remarkable McLean Hospital research scientists, opening new doors to outcomes assessment for my field and for me to discover after I had jumped of the cliff with my declaration to our service chiefs. We began their use on hospital inpatient units and became able to report on different groups of patients with different disorders, all as judged by the patients themselves.

Later we extended their use to McLean outpatient services, created as part of our growth strategy to both diversify services and allow for continuing care, when possible.

PROOF

In 1995 (against baseline data collected from 1986 to 1992), we sampled 1,581 McLean patients to assess their clinical improvement. This analysis demonstrated that these (adult) respondents showed significant reductions in all five of the BASIS-32 domains: relation to self/others, daily living skills, depression/anxiety, impulsive/addictive, and psychosis.

In other words, McLean clinical services were doing their job, helping our patients recover from their symptoms and function better in their lives. These gains were achieved despite the substantial lessening of inpatient stays—and the admission of a far broader and diverse population of patients. McLean was no longer selecting who would be admitted, as it had for so many years. We were done with the past admission hurdles that had been a deterrent to admission.

Our 1995 sample showed generally low scores of difficulties (1–2+ on a 4-point scale), though higher than ratings from previous years. Seriously ill psychiatric patients often underreport their degrees of difficulty. This was especially true of people with psychotic conditions, who, when acutely ill, often lack insight into their problems and may attribute them to outside forces or other people. This trait applied as well to those with serious character disorders, like borderline personality, who project blame and accountability onto others. Patients, nevertheless, reported improvements from admission to discharge. We paid special attention to the delta, the degree of improvement they reported from their baseline.

The results of our analyses of patient self-reported symptoms and functioning were additional, important validation that we were on mission. These data analyses were presented at board meetings and to our clinical staff, those who had done the work.

We were able to pair quantitative assessments and changes by using the BASIS-32, with our customary assessments by McLean's doctors, nurses, and other professional and nonprofessional staff. But not without risk: the standardized use of the BASIS-32 could reveal, in the opinions of our patients, whether this Harvard teaching hospital was or was not providing effective clinical care. Its results were a part of *McLean Reports*, previously mentioned, which we published quarterly and distributed widely within McLean and to thousands of others in our professional communities.

VOICE, CLARITY, AND DIGNITY

Hospitals and many other organizations have employed patient satisfaction surveys for many years. For example: How was the food? The accommodations? Wait times to be seen at emergency rooms were still to come. The McLean Hospital we aspired to rebuild would go further, seeking ways for patients to give voice to their experiences of the care they received at McLean. Were they treated with respect and dignity? Were they given clear, understandable, and helpful information about their condition and its treatment? The PoC also used Likert-like scales to assess the degree to which we met patients' needs and expectations.

Administered consistently and with attention to the patient's responses, the PoC asked for a patient's experience in three areas:

- Interpersonal aspects of the patient/staff experience, such as did the patient feel respect and dignity was shown to them, reflections on the courtesy and friendliness of staff, and was the patient asked about their opinions and given choices about their care.

- Staff/patient communication, such as information about the patient's treatment, lab and other tests received, what the patient could expect about their care, what the patient's rights were, and information about and how their program delivered safe and effective treatment, as well as unit policies, especially about safety.

- Other aspects of inpatient psychiatric care, such as the patient's view of the coordination of their care (especially planning posthospital community care) and the patient's view of the quality and outcomes from treatment (did the patient believe they were helped and if so how?). All at the heart of achieving excellence in patient care.

Here too, as with the BASIS-32, our patients were de-identified and anonymous. And we could understand and assess what it was like to be a psychiatric patient on specific specialty units. And to consider how to make that experience better.

Were McLean patients, in their own eyes, better or worse or not changed by their treatment at McLean? And for all involved to know.

Analyses of PoC reports, also in 1995, revealed that 69 percent of the McLean patients sampled had scores of excellent/very good on whether our staff had treated them with dignity and respect, and an additional 18 percent rated their experience as good. We also achieved high scores for the courtesy and friendliness of staff (68 percent excellent/very good and 21 percent good). These two measures of quality are essential because for psychiatric care to proceed successfully, a patient must believe the caregiver is on their side, there to help them—which starts with the interpersonal moments they experience, which enables them to better join with their treatment team in the hard work of recovery.

Our PoC performance analyses also reported scores regarding the recognition of patient opinions: 51 percent excellent/very good, 24 percent good, and 20 percent fair/poor. These findings became the focus of one of our quality improvement initiatives, which resulted in inviting peers (those with mental illness and lived experience, on their own recovery road) to attend groups with inpatients, treating psychiatrists and nurses (who were better able to explain what the doctors were saying about illness and treatment, as well as answer their questions). Thank you, peers and nurses.

RESTRAINT, PRUDENT PSYCHOPHARMACOLOGY, READMISSIONS

Not incidentally, our harmful events scores showed significant improvements (reductions) in the use of restraint and seclusion.

We were able to show, as well, the prudent use of medications, especially antipsychotic medications in older patients (with greater sensitivity to higher doses).

Both of these areas of hospital performance became focused, quality-improvement projects. If you have a method that works don't forget to use it.

The data on McLean's thirty-day readmissions rate showed an increase from 6 percent to 14 percent, though we were still below the national average. And we no longer kept patients for very extended stays. Our average length of stay had dropped by 75 percent to fourteen days. Yet, our analyses showed that patients who had slightly longer stays (days to a week or more) had lower readmission rates, consistent with the severity of their illnesses.

Moreover, higher rates of readmission did *not* result in greater annual cumulative days spent in the hospital. While we had an increase in rates of readmission, our patients had fewer total days per year spent in the hospital—which means more of their lives were lived in community and family settings. Over time, McLean demonstrated "bicameral" (two peaks on a graph) lengths of stay, some briefer, averaging twelve days, and some longer, averaging fifteen days. Some patients take (a bit) more time to recover sufficiently for discharge. I don't know how, but today, average lengths of stay in many general and community hospitals have become as low as three to seven days. A twenty-one-bed inpatient ward with a seven average stay means three discharges and three admissions every day.

SPREADING THE WORD

We received requests for the BASIS-32 from more than 600 other healthcare organizations.

In 1996, the BASIS-32 was the winner of the New England Assembly's Blue Ribbon award. Its use was being adopted by other psychiatric settings around the country.

In 1997, McLean won the National Association on Mental Illness/Johns Hopkins Outcomes Program Award.

In 1998, McLean's Performance Measurement System was approved by the Joint Commission on Accreditation of Healthcare Organizations (then the JCAHO, now simply TJC—The Joint Commission). This allowed other facilities to replicate our work while also meeting national accreditation survey requirements.

ASSESSING OUTCOMES IN PUBLIC MENTAL HEALTHCARE

I worked for New York State's (NYS) public mental health agency (OMH, the Office of Mental Health) for thirteen years, near to twelve as its chief medical officer. Our inpatient "standard" for the duration of their stay (OMH then operated 3,300 beds in twenty-two hospitals) was that patients would stay as long as needed. We saw, however, if a patient was hospitalized for one year, they tended to remain hospitalized for many years; this led us to focus the agency's work on helping patients (and families) not cross that boundary in time. Longer stays usually mean greater loss of everyday functioning (see the chapter "An Iatrogenic Disorder" earlier in this book), making adaptation to independent living harder (and lonelier).

NYS operates the largest state public hospital system in the country, short of the VA system (which of course is federal, and in all states). NYS remains a welcome outlier to all other state mental health agencies. We were proud of the standard of "staying as long as needed" but mindful of its unintended consequences. In the course of serious mental illness disorders, there can be a time when hospital care becomes necessary. But we also hewed to the adage that "as a rule, less is more."

In the past few decades, this country has seen a great diminution in public mental healthcare, once the province of state hospitals across the country. Some say this is one factor in the nationally increasing rates of homelessness. Among chronically homeless people, mental and addictive disorders are ubiquitous. But they do not necessarily need to live their lives in a state hospital, though they need safe and reliable housing; medical, mental health, and substance use treatment; and support.

QUALITY CARE

Dr. Barbara Dickey and I later coedited two textbooks on measuring and improving the clinical quality of mental health (and addiction) services. Dr. Sue Eisen continued refining and advancing her work with the BASIS-32 and the PoC, with the latter making its way into nationally supported and used clinical measurement tools.

Proven treatments properly delivered over time can, incrementally, improve the quality of the lives of people with serious mental illness (SMI) and addictive disorders, if they are done well and with continuity for one level of care to another. Performance measurement and improvement should be a standard operating procedure (SOP) in public mental health settings serving diverse groups of patients in diverse settings. People with a mental illness or addiction warrant good care wherever they are treated, in public, not only private settings. That would be good for them—and for us citizens whose taxes pay for publicly rendered treatments.

Mental health treatment works for people with SMI, when surrounded by social welfare and health supports. That takes hard work and persistent communications at every level of a system of medical care. For a hospital, it is the clerks, the aides and nurses, the doctors, social workers and psychologists, security, food and cleaning services who deliver the services and the setting that chronically ill people need to build (or rebuild) their lives.

With growing support, my conviction that McLean could and would continuously improve quality became a reality. That hewing to standards of excellence would make us all be proud we stayed the course, that we did not give up on people who by no fault of their own suffer from illnesses that can rob them of a life. That's the beacon that calls us to the transformative, radical change needed to do so.

The best moment for a clinical leader, I think, is when our colleagues—along with the entire chain of care—in the wake of their success take credit for work well done. As they should: It takes ongoing dedication—by the patient, family, and caregivers—to achieve a life of recovery for those living with a chronic mental illness.

FACTS ECLIPSE SPECULATIONS

Reporting on the outcomes of McLean Hospital's performance (in many domains) proved a powerful antidote to the ongoing expressions by a few vocal but influential senior clinical staff that the Mirin administration, with me as its clinical director, was "ruining" the quality of the care that had been delivered before our time. Back when lengths of stay were sixty-three days and the cost of a day in the hospital became prohibitive. Before we established a staff professional practice, where psychiatrists and psychologists were paid by the hospital and available to immediately commence care, the search for a private doctor became history. The hospital paid staff psychiatrists for their time and services, so they could be blind to the hugely variable (though mostly low) fees paid by third parties.

Critics are not entitled to deny the reality of what was benefi-
cially happening at McLean Hospital. Our board and clinical and
administrative leadership had ongoing, credible data to support
the value of the relentless transformation underway at McLean.
We were doing clinical work differently, and it made a measurable
difference for the better.

PRIDE

For a few years, *McLean Reports* was sent to 40,000 recipients (by
mail and fax; this was before the internet). We printed it. Usually,
it was on the agenda at McLean board meetings, where Mirin or
I would present recent, pertinent material from *McLean Reports*.
Those were moments of shared pride, during the stormy years
of change.

It was a great personal accomplishment for me to have led the
installation of a reliable, quality measurement system, rooted in
the views held by patients, and sensitive to change with two-week
stays, sometimes less. We showed that we counted what counted,
all the more meaningful as we also blended in administrative data,
regulatory compliance, patient outcomes, and their experience
of the care provided. It's awfully hard to "game" comprehensive
results from multiple sources. The doubters were entitled to how
they felt (a concept I learned from my other great boss, Dr. Michael
Hogan), but they did not have the data to support their publicly
stated contentions. We were on track, on mission, they were left
behind, not because of the people in the yellow brick building, but
by their own doing.

McLean would soon regain its stature, not be prey to being
closed or taken over, and continue to serve so many people and
their families into the future.

PS: Later, after I left McLean, I coedited another quality book, though not with Barbara Dickey. I now have published three books on quality measurement and improvement in mental healthcare, all learned by on-the-job training with brilliant experts and dedicated clinical staff. So can you.

Writing sharpens the mind, demands clarity, humanity, and brevity whenever possible, and should eschew all jargon. These books would stand me well in the three jobs I have had subsequent to McLean. I imagine this work was instrumental to my recruitment in 2002 as mental health commissioner for New York City, under its new mayor, Michael Bloomberg.

14

MOVING ON

"To be acknowledged… is {to be} overpaid."

—*King Lear* (Shakespeare)

I was in my customary outer row seat at the McLean board meeting when its chair, the distinguished George Putnam, passed on the mantle of chair to John Kaneb, a self-made man. Mr. Kaneb, knowing fully the grim circumstances of the hospital, and the work it would take to save it, remarked (and I paraphrase), "Putnam knows when to get in and when to get out."

John Kaneb was an anchor for McLean and our leadership team in those years of tumult and worry. Steven Mirin knew that Kaneb had his back (his "six"), so long as team Mirin was taking all the necessary steps to first staunch the financial bleeding, and second to create McLean's next, fulsome chapter in its storied history. And we did.

CHANGE OF GUARD

Then, in 1997, when the clinical, research, training, and financial projections for the hospital were all trending well, Mirin decided to leave. He had been in the psychiatrist in chief post, vacated by his inimitable predecessor and mentor, Shervert Frazier, MD, for eight long years.

Mirin had led the transformation and recovery of McLean, Harvard's only psychiatric hospital, to then take a job in Washington, DC, as medical director of the American Psychiatric Association. He asked me if I wanted to join him, leading the clinical services division of the APA. I was greatly moved by his invitation. But I said, no thanks. Not at that time. I would stay at McLean as chief medical officer, continuing to work on growing and improving clinical services to help ensure the financial and clinical recovery we had achieved.

I asked Dr. Mirin if it would be okay for me to talk with a senior member of the McLean Board, in light of Mirin's leaving. We met at the hospital. I was still needed at McLean, I was kindly told, to see our effective changes through, which was what I thought as well.

I stayed. I continued as the CMO and executive vice president of the hospital. Even in a tempest everyone needs to feel valued, not expendable. It helps to have evidence that you are sought elsewhere. That seems to be in the nature of most institutions, though I wouldn't suggest it for marriage.

The wrinkle in Mirin leaving, as I touched on earlier in this book, was, of course, who would replace him as president and psychiatrist in chief. To many, I seemed the front-runner.

SUCCESSION

The board went about its process for selecting McLean's next psychiatrist leader. It seemed to drag on and on. I had no phone call from the powers deciding who would be the hospital's next psychiatrist in chief. Being in the dark left me perplexed and anxious. Do we ever fully leave behind our childhood ghosts of doubt? It was clear I did not. As a psychiatrist I should—and do—know that doubt often has deep roots that are hard to pull, even by psychiatrists themselves, like me.

I was disappointed it wasn't me. Where did I fail? Might my being passed over signal a shift, in ways we had foreclosed in our years of battle to keep McLean alive? Except that did not happen. The mind does have a mind of its own.

My lunch with the board member who had called me was at an understated membership club in Boston. It had the type of worn Persian carpets that cover the floors of many New England clubs (and some homes). At lunch, we talked about diverse careers, with their ups and downs. What I needed to do, I inferred from the most kind of stories, was to swallow my pride, try not to choke on it, then move on.

That was right, of course, knowing how and when work life changes, in many a diverse professional crucible. And how to make those moments less painful.

I have heard since then that it's wise to hire an executive who has been fired at least once (but not for any impropriety); it's best when the wounds mostly have healed. I have had my job "plug" pulled a number of times, before and after McLean (though never for misdeeds or poor performance of my job). I now get it about how pride can impede moving on, in finding an opportunity (or it finding me) to do further good.

The hardest moments for me at the hospital were when I attended a McLean function, like a dinner or fundraiser, and heaps of praise were showered on the hospital's new leader. It seemed mythmaking to me. It also was difficult when I continued to attend the weekly executive team meeting, so very different from those Mirin headed. I missed the clear, driven, and determined leadership that Dr. Steve Mirin had delivered. His humor too! But I kept my peace.

Eventually, I began to see how my influence and clinical services management were inexorably diminishing. I proposed a different role for myself at McLean. I had spent years focused on defining, measuring, and improving clinical quality in mental health and substance use disorders. I suggested that I found a clinical quality institute as part of the hospital's growing and diversified portfolio. I loved the field of quality measurement and clinical performance and improvement, where clinical, not only administrative performance, was measurable and useful— to patients, families, doctors, and nurses. I had coauthored two books on the subject with my colleague Barbara Dickey and had Susan Eisen to continue to research and develop psychiatric hospital improvement measures. But few hospitals adopted our "product"—not because of its fees. I discovered (by asking) because of its rigor; they could pass inspection with a far less demanding set of measures. But at McLean, rigor reigned. That was the point: anything else would not do.

We had the people, the goods, the track record, and the publications to start an institute. Yet, as I planned to do that, the writing on the wall grew bigger and brighter, as doors kept closing. Because it was time for me to go.

My chief medical officer leadership role also progressively diminished. For example, goals or problems I had fielded were handed off to other senior colleagues, not to me. These and other sidelining events felt like slowly removing the bandage from a wound, rather than quickly stripping it off.

For those skirting around making an important decision because they consider it kindly to wait, I can attest to the genuine (even if painful) *relief* that comes from seeing the world as it is, not as one may imagine. After not very long, I concluded that if, indeed, my fate had been decided, it could not come soon enough. I had lasted two years at McLean after Mirin left, into the next millennium. The early spring of 2000 had arrived.

I asked for a meeting with a leader from both McLean and Partners (to which the hospital then reported), which mercifully happened promptly. I thanked them for their time and asked to speak, meaning to end the small talk. I began by referencing the writing on the wall. I proposed not a quality institute, but rather three more months to transition out of my job and leave McLean Hospital, a severance commensurate with eleven years of service to McLean, which was prospering once again, and no party.

Without what seemed hardly a moment for consideration, debate, or discussion, my proposal was accepted. Relief came in stages. At first, it was as if I had surfaced from a dark sea and finally could take in a deep breath of air. But that air still was riddled with self-doubt. What had I done wrong? What had I not done to advance the hospital's recovery? Losing this job also meant losing a highly accomplished community of colleagues who had walked the walk of restoring Mclean; some had become close friends. Income too! I came to conclude that I had not done anything wrong, or shameful. I thought I was simply obsolete and in the way.

Steven Mirin was one of the first people I called. Perhaps no one could appreciate my dilemma more than him. When I called him, I don't think I had planned to ask, but out it came: Was his offer to join him at the APA still alive? Yes, it was, he said, with some changes that I might appreciate. Presto, my next landing zone. What a week that was. I was out of a job, had a new job waiting, and would promptly be moving to Washington, DC, where the APA offices were. It's funny how much freedom comes from sweeping everything off the table at once. One piece at a time can be studded with snags that hurt.

GIRL, INTERRUPTED

Let's pause for me to tell you a story from the tail end of my time at McLean Hospital, which I think portrays the hospital we had rebuilt. Few know this story, but many know its characters.

You might not have heard about Susanna Kaysen's slender 1993 book, *Girl, Interrupted*. But I imagine that many have seen or heard of its 1999 film production, with the same title.

In 1967, Susanna Kaysen, at the age of eighteen, was admitted to McLean Hospital after a very brief office evaluation and then referral to the hospital from a private practice psychiatrist friend of her parents. He considered her a danger to herself, having taken "50 aspirins," as being depressed, and "need[ing] a rest." This psychiatrist sent her to the hospital by taxi, telling the driver to "not let her out till you get there."[26]

No longer a minor, she signed herself into McLean as a "voluntary" admission—though that meant little back then in terms of liberties, no less the capacity to leave when she might have wished. She remained hospitalized for eighteen months, then was discharged. She was given the diagnosis of borderline personality disorder.

---

26   Susanna Kaysen, *Girl, Interrupted* (New York: Random House, 1993).

In 1993, four years into my job at McLean, I had immediately read the book. Ms. Kaysen told a chilling tale of psychiatric hospital oppression, and the endless, bitter battles between patients and staff. Her characters embodied the painful—and often hopelessly depicted—varieties of mental illnesses, as well as their bleak treatments.

Reading Kaysen's book left me feeling that more was needed to achieve changing the clinical culture of the hospital. The following tale happened some years later.

CULTURE CHANGE

Radically changing any institution means changing its culture. To change a culture means changing the people who give expression to that culture, a well-worn concept, more of an adage, I think, than a cliché. I was not then, nor am I today, big on didactic methods of changing people. I think we can change how we think of others, especially those who are stigmatized (as are people with mental and substance use disorders), by having direct and thus different human experiences with those whom we don't understand and may fear. Change can more readily happen when we are face-to-face, seeing a person and not a "patient" or a caricature, and by listening to their perspectives, experiences, and ideas.

So, I had the bright idea to invite Ms. Kaysen to speak at McLean, which would be our meeting with someone who had firsthand experience of McLean, and who was frank and articulate. Perhaps, I imagined, we could have an interview with her, one open to all our clinical staff. Through an intermediary, I was able to contact her. "Not interested" was her quick and definitive response, though I did try again, also to no avail. Oh well, change would need to proceed without her voice, as it did happen.

Fast-forward to 1999, six years later at McLean. We were no longer on the "endangered species" list. The nature of clinical care and the interpersonal relations between patients and staff were better, but we still could go higher. Then I saw a notice that *Girl, Interrupted* was to be released as a film.

Ah, maybe another opportunity to invite Ms. Kaysen? Perhaps the invitation would more likely be accepted, especially with the help of her agent and the commercial interests at play. Once again, through an intermediary, I reached out to her. After a brief delay, she accepted.

The film had a limited release in December 1999 (in time to qualify for the Academy Awards) and a general release in early 2000. It starred Angelina Jolie (who won an Oscar for Best Supporting Actress), Winona Ryder, Whoopi Goldberg, Vanessa Redgrave, and Elisabeth Moss.

McLean Hospital was not where it was filmed. The former Pennsylvania State Lunatic Hospital and Union Asylum (founded in 1845)—later, the Harrisburg State Hospital—was used instead. It was a far more battered campus than McLean had, but the wards were familiar: the rather bleak institutional settings they had been for decades, especially in the old and unrenovated buildings built in the 1960s and before. Moreover, the Harrisburg State Hospital had an underground series of tunnels that connected most of the buildings for transporting materials and people, as did McLean. Those tunnels can be eerie, and the film did capitalize on them.

Upon watching the film back then (and again to write this tale), I found the book to be far less histrionic, more pensive than the movie. Jolie went all out to be as wild, contentious, and in your face a person as she could be, which won her an Academy Award. Quite a few fictional additions were created for the film, which made it more (film) noir, and conveying even more hopelessness and defeat than did the book. The director James Mangold seemed determined to leave the viewer disturbed by mental illnesses, as well as with psychiatrists and nurses (with the exception of the nurse played by Whoopi Goldberg). Mangold was not forgiving, giving particular attention to portraying the oppressive conditions of a psychiatric hospital, with its staff front and center.

I thought, and imagined others would as well, that viewers would witness a darker portrayal of psychiatric care than was accurate, at least at McLean in 1999, after near to a decade spent re-creating the hospital, its programs, and its culture. The film's depiction of mental illnesses and their treatments could further the stigmatization of those affected by these conditions. Stigma erodes a person, evokes shame, and often deters someone from seeking needed and increasingly effective treatment. I invited Susanna Kaysen to an open forum at McLean. Some others on our management team had their reservations, as did I since I had no idea what to expect. But it could be a good idea. . . .

Kaysen and I agreed that she would be joined by a woman companion of her choosing. We would have a one-hour interview (followed by a Q and A) seated at a table at the very front of the glass-enclosed, well-lit, large, and modern de Marneffe cafeteria. The interview would not be recorded. Tables were removed and replaced by a lot of chairs. All McLean clinical and administrative staff were invited. The turnout was considerable, standing room only. I had never met Kaysen until she arrived that day. I did not interview her, instead asked a woman psychiatrist I admired to do so. We had drafted beforehand a set of questions and topics, which we shared with Kaysen.

Kaysen's life after her McLean stay became a lot better, she said. She had no further hospital admissions. She continued to write. As she details in the last chapter of her book, her relationships with men remained troubled. In the interview, she was very thoughtful in her commentary about her eighteen-month experience at McLean, not at all bitter. She gave us a window into how a person with a mental illness rebuilds their life: by reflecting and making sense of the sometimes-strange workings of our mind, by developing and sustaining relationships that were supportive to her, by finding purpose, and by staying the course that recovery demands, as it does from all chronic disorders.

While she was careful not to comment openly, I (for one) thought she was not keen on the movie.

One question (and answer) that still lingers in my mind was "In all, what did she think of McLean and its clinical staff?" She said, and I paraphrase, her best experiences were with the nurses and some aides. Thank you, Ms. Kaysen. We doctors can and should learn from nurses. They need to be better supported and recognized for all they do if we want to retain them in our hospitals, not ignore or dismiss them, all the more so after the COVID pandemic.

There were few questions from the audience. The time passed quickly. Chairs stirred and the exodus back to work ensued. I was grateful for her visit, and told her so, mostly for me than her, I suspect. I admired her courage and intelligence, but that would have been gratuitous to say to her. Maybe she will have occasion to read this story. I hope so.

The book's (and film's) title derives from the Johannes Vermeer painting *Girl Interrupted at Her Music* (c. 1658). As had Kaysen's life been interrupted when mental illness entered in her teenage years, and she then lived in a mental hospital for eighteen months. As dark as those days surely must have been, she writes at the very end of her book that she saw "another sort of light, the fitful, overcast light of life, in which we see ourselves and others only imperfectly . . ." Light, not darkness, nevertheless.

BACK TO MY GOOD NEWS

My next landing zone would not be as alien or unwelcome, as
it had been at McLean. The future of the APA was not perilous,
as it had been at McLean. I was taking on a different job, not
more of the same. Change is a tonic. I would see how I could do
contributing to a very different organization, with a different, if
overlapping, mission.

McLean would soon evaporate from my life, with its brimming
energy that had fueled so much change, and with its bucolic setting
on the Frederick Olmsted-designed campus in Belmont, Massachusetts. My diminished role at the hospital had been underway; it's just
that I had been wearing a blindfold. Into my box of memories went
the 246 acres, the garden of decorative trees, and the truly astound-
ing talented and driven colleagues I had the privilege to work with.
After eleven years of driving onto McLean's estate-like grounds
and looking out from the perch of the Administration Building, I
knew the DC urban terrain would be very different. I was diving off
another cliff, which simultaneously created the wonderful feeling
of being weightless and the dread of where and how I would land.

I was the only one of our executive team who threw himself
under McLean's moving bus. I was the only one who needed to
go, now that Steven Mirin was gone. It seemed that my work,
my portfolio, was divided among three senior clinical staff. I don't
think it was just that I had a big workload, but rather not letting
too much influence and power reside in one person.

As I gathered and mustered some perspective, I could see that it
was not me but the hospital that was moving on. I had not changed:
A person's character, mine included, is rather fixed, like the etched
coins of ancient Greece. I became stationary while the set was in
motion, like when a film actor poses with the backdrop changing. It
was time for me to get off the set and go someplace else.

I too discovered, not for the first time or the last, T. S. Eliot's message. His "note to self":[27]

> *And the end of all our exploring*
>
> *Will be to arrive where we started*
>
> *And know the place for the first time.*

Though seasoned by circumstances, sweet and sour, drawn from heaven and hell, I remained fundamentally who I am. T. S. Eliot's "place" was mine too.

PS: By the way, there was a going-away party, small, private, and lovely, held at a close friend and colleague's home. It felt more like a birthday party, noting yet another year of my passage.

---

27   Christopher Ricks and Jim McCue, eds, *The Poems of T. S. Eliot: Collected and Uncollected Poems, Volume 1* (Baltimore: Johns Hopkins University Press, 2015); Christopher Ricks and Jim McCue, eds, *The Poems of T. S. Eliot: Practical Cats and Further Verses, Volume 2* (Baltimore: Johns Hopkins University Press, 2015).

ACKNOWLEDGMENTS

SUCCESS in virtually all human service endeavors calls for team play, which in turn calls for a leader on a mission, with a moral compass, who builds a band of die-hards, enlists trustworthy support, and knows to persevere.

I have been on several teams that aimed to improve our world and did so in ways to be proud of. I am grateful for their leadership, who delivered on commonsense, and their unyielding pursuit of mission, clarity, and honesty. A sense of humor also comes in handy.

My pantheon of personal leaders includes those for whom I have worked and those who are beacons in the night. Among the bosses are Dr. Michael Hogan, former commissioner of mental health for New York State; Michael Bloomberg, former mayor of New York City; and Dr. Steven Mirin, former psychiatrist in chief of McLean Hospital (whom you met throughout this book) and, later, a former medical director of the American Psychiatric Association.

A great teacher who gave inspiration and set standards for my thinking and writing is Mr. William Zinsser, now deceased, but who continues to inhabit my head in his tender, demanding, and Yankee way. To my great friend, Francis Greenburger, for his humanity and undaunted pursuit of social justice. While I have had many book editors, the two at the top are Deborah Malmud for my first book for a general audience, and Nathan True for ensuring I give you a compelling, meaningful, yet personal story (his fingerprints are all over this book).

My absolute *true north* is my wife, Rosanne Haggerty. Her values, integrity, ideals, grit, and faith are a wonder to behold.

Lloyd I. Sederer, MD
Concord, New Hampshire

ABOUT THE AUTHOR

LLOYD I. SEDERER, MD, is a psychiatrist, public health doctor, and nonfiction writer. He is an adjunct professor at Columbia University Mailman School of Public Health, who has been Chief Medical Officer and Executive Vice President of McLean Hospital, a Harvard teaching hospital; Mental Health Commissioner of New York City (in the Bloomberg administration); and Chief Medical Officer of the New York State Office of Mental Health, the nation's largest state mental health agency.

He has published fourteen books, the first seven for medical professionals (two with multiple editions) and, more recently, six for a general audience. He has published hundreds of articles in print and online publications, including the *New York Times*, the *Wall Street Journal*, *Scientific American*, *Psychology Today*, *Lancet*, *Medscape*, *The Atlantic*, *The Tennessean*, *Commonwealth*, and *U.S. News and World Report* (where he wrote an opinion column for three years). He was medical editor for mental health at *HuffPost*, where he wrote and published articles, audio reports, and videos.

His awards include the Rockefeller Scholar in Residence, Doctor of the Year from the National Council on Behavioral

Health, both Administrator and Teacher of the Year (in different years) from the American Psychiatric Association, the Dutch Psychiatric Association's Certificate of Honor, and The Courage to Change from the New York State Association of Psychiatric Rehabilitation Services.

He founded and provided a workshop on medical writing for the general public at the Columbia Department of Psychiatry, where he also founded and directed Columbia Psychiatry Media. He has begun leading a faculty workshop on writing for the general public at the Columbia University Mailman School of Public Health.

Dr. Sederer lives in Concord, New Hampshire, with his wife and dog.

Please visit www.askdrlloyd.com.